FREE THE IDEA MONKEY...

...to focus on what matters most!

G. MICHAEL MADDOCK
with RAPHAEL LOUIS VITÓN
as the (Ring)leader

**For the Priceless People
who can magically create
Big Ideas and the special
few who can actually
manaqe them.**

Dallas • Atlanta • Nashville • Los Angeles

FREE THE IDEA MONKEY...
to focus on what matters most!

ISB Publishing
2128 Boll Street
Dallas, TX 75204 USA

ISBN 978-1-93648-710-3

CREDITS

Managing Editor:	Lisa Grimenstein
Jacket Design:	G. Michael Maddock
Illustrations:	Wesley E. Douglas
	G. Michael Maddock
	Chris Miller
Type Design:	Deanne DiVito

Get real tools to empower the Idea Monkey and inspire the (Ring)leader.

Go to http://freetheideamonkey.com/treasurehunt and type in the passcode WONDERMONKEY for the free gift* that will help you empower and inspire the Idea Monkeys and (Ring)leaders in your life.

*While supplies last. We have no idea how many of you people are actually going to want these things.

For our kids:
Gunnar, Cody, Rosy, Raffi and Spencer

Acknowledgments

Thanks to the many people—clients and teammates—who have helped create our unmatched Agency of Innovation® services. We are grateful for your hard work, for your curiosity and for the inventive mojo you share with the world every day.

One of our core values at Maddock Douglas is "ideas from anywhere." Our company has grown because of the hard work and dedication of MD team members, past and present, whose fingerprints are all over this book. Thank you all for helping to create a platform that inspires and empowers curious people.

There are some MD peeps that contributed directly to this effort. Special thanks to Jim Campbell, Caroline Courtois, Deanne DiVito, Javier Flaim, Paul Grachan, Frank Grubich, Brett Miller, Stephanie Savage, Doug Stone, Maria Umbach, Luisa Uriarte and McRae Williams. While many were tempted to run when they saw us coming, you bravely stood your ground and leaned into adversity.

Thanks also to George and Nancy Maddock and Rafael and Barbara Vitón. Now that we're parents too, our goal is to instill an indestructible sense of wonder and a hard work ethic that makes witnessing serendipity much more likely. You folks gave us these gifts and we're eternally grateful.

Finally, we thank our beautiful brides Ruth and Kelly for their encouragement, laughter and hugs. You are two seriously hot mommas.

Most respectfully,

Mike & Raff

Table of Contents

(Fail) Foreword

DO-IT-YOURSELF ASTRONAUTS; IDEA MONKEYS AND YOU

Larry Walters had always wanted to fly, but poor eyesight kept him from becoming an Air Force pilot. So to make his dream come true, he got creative.

The equation was pretty simple:

$$\begin{aligned}
& \textbf{Balloons} \\
+\ & \textbf{Lawn Chair} \\
+\ & \textbf{Beer} \\
=\ & \textbf{Flying Fun}
\end{aligned}$$

Larry acquired (I haven't a clue how) 45 weather balloons and filled them with helium. Then he attached the balloons to his favorite aluminum lawn chair that, for the time being, he had tied to his Jeep.

He reasoned that he could float above his backyard for awhile in what he decided to call *Inspiration I*, have a few beers and then shoot the balloons with a pellet gun so that he could descend gently back down.

Like most brilliant idea people, Larry believed that overcomplicating his concept with unnecessary details—such as asking what could go wrong—was a waste of time. He was an activator and it was time to fly. He grabbed a bunch of sandwiches, a six-pack, his pellet gun and a camera. He untethered the lawn chair and ...

(Cue the something-bad-is-about-to-happen music.)

At this point things started to veer from Larry's unplanned plan. *Inspiration I* rose rapidly to 16,000 feet—that's more than three miles above the earth. He was too afraid to shoot a balloon because he thought he might unbalance the chair and fall out.

His chair soon floated through the primary approach corridor of Long Beach Airport, causing pilots to question whether they were losing their minds as they looked at a guy with a six-pack and a pellet gun float by in what appeared to be a lawn chair.

After 45 minutes in the sky, he got up the nerve to shoot several balloons, but then accidentally dropped his pellet gun overboard. Whoopsy!

Eventually the balloons lost enough helium so that his spacecraft descended far enough to become entangled in Long Beach power lines, which caused a neighborhood blackout for 20 minutes. Whoopsy 2!

Larry climbed down to the ground where he was arrested and fined $4,000 for violating federal aviation regulations. He received the top prize from the Bonehead Club of Dallas as well as an honorable mention in the Darwin Awards ("Honoring those who improve the species ... by accidentally removing themselves from it!").

Frankly, he was lucky to be alive.

When I first heard it, I found the story of Larry Walters' adventure incredibly amusing. What a knucklehead. But as I was writing this book, something occurred to me that made my skin crawl.

I AM LARRY WALTERS AND, PERHAPS, SO ARE YOU

Like most entrepreneurs, I have lots of ideas. But like Larry's, my ideas are not always considered practical by the poor souls who will have to actually execute them.

Some people, like me, keep their ideas to themselves, which is sad. Some go off half-cocked and crash their businesses or their lives—which is even sadder.

Then there are the Idea Monkeys like you and me who have discovered that we aren't all that great at this "channeling ideas" thing. We need some help, and this book was written to provide it.

If you are an Idea Monkey, then you will learn how to use your superhero powers for good, not evil. You will learn how to focus on what matters, lead the people who need leading and have what others consider to be better ideas.

If you are the person who manages the Idea Monkey, you are the (Ring)leader—the young lady working so hard on the cover of this book. The book will make your life easier. You'll learn how to motivate and guide the Monkey to work with laser focus on the things that matter the most. You'll come away with an even bigger unfair competitive advantage.

In either case, you will be more productive and have more fun, although perhaps not quite as much fun as Larry Walters did. (But then again, you won't be risking your life.)

Be Wonder-Full!

Mike

Mike Maddock

Chapter 1

Free the Idea Monkey

"I have an idea!"

This simple phrase can set you on a course for either world domination or complete and utter failure. It turns out that having an idea is easy. But making ideas happen is far trickier.

This book was written for two reasons: I—a card-carrying Idea Monkey myself—want to help you, the brainstorming, high-energy, big idea person who feels the strongest when solving the world's biggest—and most miniscule—challenges. You are the one who I fondly refer to as the "Idea Monkey." And Idea Monkeys need to be saved ... from themselves. It was also written for those people who have the extremely challenging—and underappreciated—job of managing them.

ARE YOU AN IDEA MONKEY? TAKE THE QUIZ

We were all born Idea Monkeys, but most of us are no longer. For that sad fact you can blame knowledge, fear, pragmatism, experience or whatever else you like. Rather than spend a whole bunch of time pointing fingers, I'd rather spend the better part of this book helping you rediscover the Idea Monkey within. But just in case you think you don't need help, take the simple quiz that follows.

1. Can you generate at least 20 ways to create a flying hamster inside of 30 seconds? (Y) (N)

2. Do you build on others' ideas to the point they tell you to take a moment to inhale because you seem winded? (Y) (N)

3. Are you completely unconcerned that your next idea might get you fired? (Y) (N)

4. Did an idea ever get you—or almost get you—fired? (Y) (N)

5. Have you made a career out of advancing one great idea after another? (Y) (N)

6. In school, did you spend a lot of time in detention because teachers thought your daydreaming was irrelevant? (Y) (N)

7. Are you convinced that if you were a kid today, you would be medicated? (Y) (N)

8. Did you have a nickname like Einstein, Curious George, Space Cadet, Dream Weaver or Mojo Moheto as a kid? (That last one was just to see if you were paying attention.) (Y) (N)

9. Did you take your stuff apart as a kid regardless of whether you believed you could actually put it back together? (Y) (N)

10. Do you still stop today and look at leaves, bugs and blades of grass? (Y) (N)

11. When you smell freshly cut grass, are you grateful for the sun and rain that helped it grow? (Y) (N)

12. Have you made a business out of taking ideas other people just talk about and actually doing something with them? (Y) (N)

This test isn't scientific. But if you answered "yes" to at least five of the above, you may just be an Idea Monkey. If you answered "yes" to all of the above, please let me know what prison you are in so I can send you a nail file or something useful.

Or maybe you were once an Idea Monkey, but something changed you along the way and you banished your inner Idea Monkey to the attic, basement or wherever it is you put things you think are part of your past.

That occurs an awful lot. We've all heard the story about what happens to creativity once we start school. Ask any first grade class to raise their hands if they can dance, draw and sing, and all the hands go up. By the fifth grade, the same question will result in a few hands, a few laughs and a lot of snickers.

Have you lost your Idea Monkey?

Some would call this reality setting in. I call it Monkey genocide. Okay, I am being overly dramatic, but this is the opening chapter and I need you to keep reading because a) whether you are (or once were) an Idea Monkey, or b) you manage Idea Monkeys, this book is for you.

How do I know? As I said, I am one of you. I manage Idea Monkeys for a living—the company I founded and run, Maddock Douglas, is a global innovation leader (that is not me bragging; we've been hired by 25 percent of the Fortune 100 to help them innovate)—I am an Idea Monkey myself, and, more importantly, I know what it is to have someone try to banish my creativity and individuality. It began in grade school. The first day of fifth grade at St. Joseph's Catholic School in Homewood, Illinois, to be exact.

G. Michael Maddock
Age 11

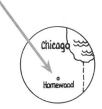

I CAN'T TEACH THIS MONKEY!

Sister Helen had us sitting at attention for roll call. (Really, she would have had us standing at attention, but the boys fidgeted too much.)

As the "M"s approached, I began to anticipate proudly announcing that the rest of the class was indeed graced with my presence.

For the record, I was a pretty good kid and generally liked by teachers and classmates, but I wasn't much of a student. I spent most of my time doodling, daydreaming and trying to crack up my friends. School was not my thing and my parents knew it. They both had been great students, so I'm pretty sure they were seriously concerned about my future, but both were charmed by my antics and believed wholly in the power of prayer. (One of the reasons, I am sure, they sent me to Catholic school.) If prayer didn't work, there was always guilt, but that's a completely different book.

CLASS RULES (you are expected to know these)

1. You may NOT interrupt <
2. You may NOT whisper <
3. You may NOT touch one another <
4. You may NOT come to class "unwashed" <
5. You may NOT switch from your assigned seats <
6. You cannot wear anything but your uniforms <
7. There will be NO swearing <
8. There will be NO yelling <
9. You may NOT read anything but assigned material... < you may NOT work on anything but what is being taught

Even before the first class began, I could tell Sister Helen didn't mess around. Her room was impeccable; the blackboard had been washed; the chalk was centered; the picture of the Pope and Jesus were at eye level and perfectly square; her habit was pressed. I imagined that this was what my dad's time in the military was like and that she fashioned herself a general for Jesus.

"A complete list of class rules is posted behind me, and you are expected to know and follow each and every one of them, otherwise you will be given a detention."

Right about here, I knew I was in trouble. As she started going over the rules, I couldn't help but comment (at least to myself) in a way destined to get myself in trouble.

- - - - - - - - -> Would now be a good time to raise my hand?

- - - - - - - - -> "What did she say?" I whispered.

- - - - - - - - -> "I bet if I slump down far enough I could kick Joey McBride's butt who is sitting in front of me. There's no way kicking is the same as touching."

- - - - - - - - -> Cue obligatory, dramatic sniff of the armpits.

- - - - - - - - -> Fine, I will move my whole desk.

- - - - - - - - -> Start planning after-school tie-dye party.

- - - - - - - - -> Memo to self: start practice on coughing the word "crap."

- - - - - - - - -> Practice coughing "crap" really loud.

- - - - - - - - -> This is about the time I picked up doodling.

You get the picture. Sister Helen believed in rigid, unbending discipline. From my seat, it looked like she had been doing it for 300 years. Also from my seat, as we saw from my (thankfully) unexpressed comments, every rule was an opportunity to bend, change or invent another reality. This kind of stuff starts early. I think that now is an important time to note that in the Middle East they believe a rebellious child is an intelligent one. Hey, do they eat Monkeys in the Middle East? I digress.

Given all these rules, I thought it might take awhile to demonstrate my individuality (despite all the subversive comments going through my head). I was wrong.

It was finally time for my name to be called during role call. I was excited. From behind her pulpit—seriously, she had a pulpit—Sister Helen called out "George Maddock?"

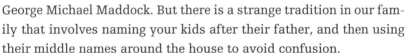

She looked around for a raised hand, cleared her throat and called out again, "GEORGE MADDOCK?"

I come from a short line of George Maddocks. My grandfather and dad are both George Maddocks. In truth, so was I: George Michael Maddock. But there is a strange tradition in our family that involves naming your kids after their father, and then using their middle names around the house to avoid confusion.

So, my name is Mike. In fact, the first time she called out for George Maddock, it didn't even register she was talking about me. By the time she broke her own rule and yelled it, my head was spinning; feelings of fight or flight were in full force.

Since I did not yet understand the concept of "winning the battle and losing the war," I decided to fight. I hoped God, my parents and the next Maddock kid to get Sister Helen as a teacher would understand. I decided I would not respond until she called me "Mike" Maddock.

While I waited, I began to whistle nervously and gaze around the room. Eventually Sister Helen noticed. Before I knew it, she was in my face.

"George Maddock?" she asked. (She smelled like Listerine.)

I continued to whistle.

"GEORGE MADDOCK?!" she demanded. (Listerine mixed with Sanka.)

"My name is Mike," I stated flatly. I was mad. How does she not know my name? It wasn't my first year in the school. My throat was beginning to constrict and my eyes were welling up, but I wasn't going to have someone—even if she was a nun—convince me that I did not know my own name. A guy has to have his dignity.

"Your name is George Maddock, and you will answer to your name! Is that clear?"

"NO!" I took a deep breath and said, very slowly, and with great emphasis, "My…name…is…MIKE. MIKE Maddock."

That was it. I was done talking to her until she called me by my name. I clammed up and stared at a fascinating piece of skin on my right index finger.

At this point she turned really red. I mean really red. It was clear we had moved beyond whatever punishment I was going to get for disobeying a rule. I started wondering what happened to 11-year-old boys who give nuns a heart attack.

"We'll see what Sister Nancy has to say about THIS!" Sister Helen bellowed as she grabbed my arm and dragged me toward the door. (Author's note: Nuns are unbelievably strong. I'm pretty sure I still have bruises on my arm. I don't know if this Herculean strength is connected to righteous might, sexual repression or the Vatican-sponsored weight room, but you don't want to mess with these ladies. Trust me.)

Sister Nancy was our principal. She was different than all the other nuns. She always wore business suits, always seemed interested in us kids and was always smiling. Every day she would walk the halls and talk to everyone she saw. She had not spoken to me yet, but I'd seen her stop and talk to my friends about their weekends, hobbies, interests. She really seemed quite un-nunlike. Sister Nancy was nice. But she was still a nun and I was still in trouble.

So there I was, sitting in Sister Nancy's reception area fighting back tears. I could feel my heart pounding in my face as I played with a thread on my hand-me-down (from my older brother Bill) uniform pants. Sister Helen stared straight ahead. I think she was growling, but I can't be sure.

Sister Nancy came out of her office, smiled at me (did she just glare at Sister Helen?) and asked us to come in.

"Good morning, Mr. Maddock." (Gulp, she knows my name!) "Tell me, Sister Helen, what opportunity have you brought me this lovely Monday morning?"

Sister Helen fixed her cold, blue eyes on me. She cleared her throat, gritted her teeth and did indeed growl, "This young man, George Maddock, refuses to answer to his name. I have told him that in my class, you must answer to your name. He does not seem to understand how to follow rules."

I never looked up from my pants thread. Surely they could see I was working on something important and would leave me alone. "Mr. Maddock," Sister Nancy said gently, "Why aren't you responding to your name?"

I wish I could tell you that I was strong enough to recite my own little declaration of independence, and explain that Sister Helen's rules were stupid and a person had a right to be called whatever they like. Or that I talked about our family's tradition of naming kids, and how while I was proud of being named for my dad and grandfather, I was still my own person. But the truth is, I could barely keep it together. Through quivering lips and tear-filled eyes, I said, "Because my name is Mike."

Sister Nancy nodded knowingly. She'd seen this type of situation—and stubbornness—before. She turned to my teacher and said sternly, "Sister Helen, you will call this young man Mike. Do you understand me?"

Sister Helen was stunned. She looked at me, then at Sister Nancy, then at a thread on her perfectly pressed habit. "Yes, Sister Nancy."

"Good. Mike, please stop by and see me anytime, and let me know how you are enjoying school."

I could not believe it. In an instant, Sister Nancy—the school's highest authority figure—had made it okay to stand up for an idea.

I didn't know it at the time, but this moment would become pivotal in my life. I realize now that it helped me continue on a path of questioning convention and authority. It helped me understand that if you believed enough in your ideas, eventually someone else would too. It helped me later on when I started my own business, to look for leaders who knew how to embrace and motivate thinkers, dreamers and idealists. Most importantly, I was seeing for the first time a tenet that most Idea Monkeys and (Ring)leaders can never fully embrace:

having rules without imagination is just as dangerous as having imagination without rules.

(Ring)leaders ~~Wanted~~ Needed

MONKEYS ARE OFTEN DIVERGENT THINKERS

Idea Monkeys often seem to have the ability to ideate with little regard for the hurdles or consequences associated with their ideas. This is because they are often highly gifted in the area of divergent thinking. According to the Gale Encyclopedia of Childhood & Adolescence, the concept of divergent thinking was developed in the 1950s by psychologist J. P. Guilford in the course of studying creative people. According to Guilford, there were important characteristics found in divergent thinkers:

Fluency
(the ability to rapidly produce a large number of ideas or solutions to a problem)

Flexibility
(the capacity to consider a variety of approaches to a problem simultaneously)

Originality
(the tendency to produce ideas different from those of most other people)

Elaboration
(the ability to think through the details of an idea and carry it out)…to the point where there isn't any more room…

(Author's note: this last trait is the rarest of them all.) Guilford would likely have taken issue with Sister Helen's rigidity. Since his research focused on testing and measurement (psychometrics), he believed that creative thinkers were at a disadvantage when it came to intelligence tests, which penalize divergent thinking and rewarded convergent thinking.

Convergent thinking
(loosely defined as one's ability to narrow down to a single solution from lots of possibilities)

As you can tell by now, I am a big believer in Idea Monkeys—the folks who, on demand, will gladly produce a stream of ideas on just about any topic without worrying about the consequences (see sidebar on divergent thinking). To some, the phrase, "Hey, Idea Monkey, get in here. We're trying to figure something out," would be offensive. To me it is the ultimate compliment.

Idea Monkeys are connectors, readily joining numerous thoughts into new ones. Unlike most people, they are able to temporarily ignore the myriad of reasons why an idea might not work and instead choose to pour their energy into possibilities. Idea Monkeys are often the energizing sparks in the room who keep ideas coming at a rapid pace. For Idea Monkeys, anything is achievable and every challenge is merely an idea waiting to happen.

For the Idea Monkey, the word "can't" is like a rallying cry for ideas. I'll never forget being in a brainstorm with a client when one of their biggest thinkers said that something could not be done. Moments later, the CEO of a wireless surveillance company—an outside expert we had asked to participate in the ideation (see Chapter 4 for why this is an important idea)—was drawing his idea for how to overcome the "can't." Our client sat dumbfounded as he recognized that he was wrong and that a solution existed. He had been concentrating on the wrong issues. Later, our client confided in me that they had been working on that challenge for five years.

Someone who knows how to awaken and manage the Idea Monkey in their organization is a (Ring)leader, an incredibly valuable resource. If you can awaken the Idea Monkey inside yourself, *you* become a priceless resource.

Idea Monkeys, as the classic Apple commercial stated, are the "Crazy Ones." They are artists, inventors, engineers and scientists. They are dreamers and believers. The Apple commercial ends with the phrase, "Because people who are crazy enough to think that they can change the world, usually do." Apple is clearly run by a bunch of Monkeys.

The Apple ad featured brief clips of these wonderful Idea Monkeys:	Albert Einstein	Thomas Edison	Alfred Hitchcock
	Bob Dylan	Muhammad Ali	Martha Graham
	Martin Luther King, Jr.	Ted Turner	Jim Hensen with
	Richard Branson	Maria Callas	Kermit the Frog
	John Lennon	Mahatma Gandhi	Frank Lloyd Wright
	R. Buckminster Fuller	Amelia Earhart	Pablo Picasso

Conversely, I believe most nuns can't innovate because they don't allow themselves to question authority. Most organizations can't innovate because they do not recognize the value of an Idea Monkey and understand how to manage their special kind of magic. As a rule, they are not led by people like Sister Nancy. Unfortunately, the Sister Helens of the world are typically in charge.

WHERE WE ARE HEADING: BE THE MONKEY, FREE THE MONKEY, HELP THE MONKEY

This section is for (Ring)leaders—the people who manage the Idea Monkeys

If you are the least bit skeptical, by now you figure I am just going to find any smart, creative person, label him or her an Idea Monkey and be done with it. Well, this book is really about you and the people you need to manage.

The thesis of this book is that you were once an Idea Monkey and that you will have a better life, a more successful career and a more profitable business if you learn how to become one again. For now, just trust me that there is a Monkey inside you begging to get out in a way that does not resemble that graphically gory scene from *Alien*. This book will start by helping you unshackle the Monkey within. Then we'll make it easy to identify the Monkeys all around you. Finally, we'll get to work teaching you how to manage an Idea Monkey-based business, because when you master the Monkey, you will spend your time focusing on the ideas that matter. You will actually see ideas through to their completion and will have a positive impact on your company, friends and, yes, even nuns.

As I watch my children create characters in the front yard, it occurs to me that Idea Monkeys have their own set of talents, beliefs and practices that they naturally orchestrate while building the best ideas. The list below describes some of the unique abilities that they have. We'll cover each in the chapters ahead so that not only can you see exactly how they do it but learn how you can do it as well.

They Have 10-D Vision. Idea Monkeys have the ability to see the world through multiple lenses. Perspective is like wonder—you tend to lose it with experience. Monkeys do the opposite. They actually develop the ability—either through practice or empathy—to view every situation through different lenses. In children, we call this imagination. In adults, we call this rare.

They Love Joyriding. When was the last time you looked forward to going to work? Idea Monkeys do because they never miss the opportunity to make even the most mundane task into an adventure. See that person smiling in the meeting? He's a Monkey.

Failforwardness Is a Good Thing. "Whoops, that didn't work, did it?" This type of statement followed by a giant smile is an everyday occurrence for an Idea Monkey. Failing is just part of the journey and a step toward figuring things out. Edison was so famous for failing that it almost became a cliché. Do you fear failure, or have you made it part of your everyday practice?

They Understand the Difference Between Knowing and Learning ... and have become learners. Perhaps the trickiest of all the Idea Monkey traits is maintaining the ability to constantly learn, even when you are the Head Monkey (otherwise known as the Leader). We often make the mistake of believing that as Leaders we need to be experts. We think, incorrectly, that expertise is measured by how much we know rather than how we learn. Monkeys are all about focusing on what they don't know, not on showing us what they already know.

They Can Produce Ideas on Demand. Being fearless and delivering new concepts anywhere, anytime is the trademark skill of the Idea Monkey. By itself, it can be received as a parlor trick. Ideas by themselves are useless. But delivered in combination under the watchful eye of a great (Ring)leader, this trait has the ability to literally change your industry.

They See the Upside of Challenges. There always will be a competitor who does the unexpected and upends your market; you can bet in the coming months consumers are going to demand something you just can't provide today, or perhaps financing that you were absolutely certain was going to be there suddenly won't be. Don't run from problems. That is what your competition will do. Find the advantage within. Idea Monkeys and Warren Buffett have a lot in common. Warren Buffett made his fortune by following an adage he came up with a long time ago: "be fearful when others are greedy—be greedy when others are fearful."

They Cross-Pollinate. All Idea Monkeys are different. But one thing they have in common is their ability to connect ideas. The reason this skill is so powerful is because the best Monkey will give credit as he makes the connections. This means that his ideas are actually your ideas too, since he will inevitably build on yours to create his.

They Leverage New Media (to start a revolution). While some fear change, the Monkey embraces it because it is new territory to explore. Today, the new frontier includes social media. This is particularly fascinating to the Idea Monkey because it plays to so many of his skills. As we will see, new media magnifies the Monkey's ability to start revolutions.

They Believe (that they can change the world). We've never met a pessimistic Idea Monkey. The ability to believe that great things are juuuuuuuuuuuuust about to happen is fundamental to most of the Monkey's superpowers.

They Find a Yin For Their Yang. We'll let you in on a little-known secret. Idea Monkeys are usually impotent (insert "yang" joke here) on their own. They need a partner to leverage their superpowers and eliminate their blind spots. The best Idea Monkeys figure this out early and look to create a dynamic duo or find or create an organization that works to leverage their skills.

They Act Like David. The biggest industries will be defeated by Idea Monkeys who are more nimble, less tied to tradition and definitely more willing to take risks (in order to gain a substantial reward). If you or your company have Goliath-like tendencies, Chapter 13 will explain what has to change (and why).

They Can Be Ruthless. By now you probably think that Idea Monkeys are the sweetest people on earth. Quite the opposite is true. The best Idea Monkeys operate with a Darwinian mindset when it comes to ideas and opportunities. They know that companies have only a limited amount of resources, and people have a finite amount of energy. That's why they only let the strongest ideas survive. They want to put their efforts behind the concepts that have the greatest chance of success.

... and behind each one of these talents should be a committed (Ring)leader ensuring laser focus and that only the best ideas survive.

They Will Take the Lead. You can either spend your time reacting to situations or shaping your environment. While Idea Monkeys are incredibly nimble, they know the odds of success increase greatly if they are the driver on the journey and not the passenger.

By the end of this book, my goals are to make you feel comfortable freeing the Idea Monkey inside you; to show you how to best channel your ideas and the ideas of your troops in order to increase the odds of success; and to give you a playbook to consult as you go forward to make sure you are getting the best work out of your people and yourself.

Let's begin.

P.S.—A HAPPY ENDING

As my eighth grade year was winding down, Sister Nancy saw me walking alone in the hall. She stopped me and asked how things were going. I told her all the different things I was excited about—and it was a long list. As I was walking away she said, "Hey, I think you're something special, George Michael," and gave me a wink. I smiled and winked back.

I am grateful for Sister Nancy's wisdom and intuition, and share her second calling of making the world a safe place for the Idea Monkey in all of us.

Go, Monkeys, go!

In the pages ahead, we will tell you how to recognize the key traits of the Idea Monkey. Then we will give you some simple ways to optimize their talents.

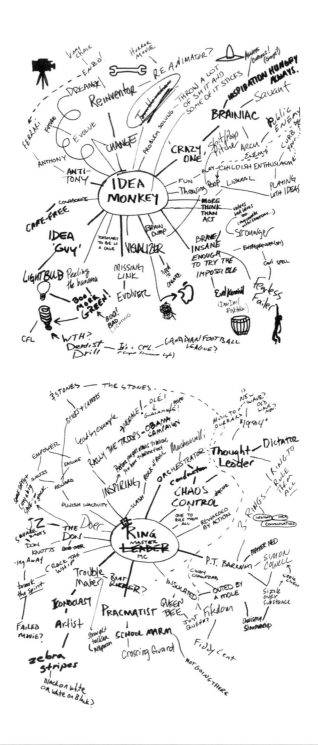

(RING)LEADER To-Dos

First: (You) take the Idea Monkey quiz. "Know thyself." Determine if you feel stronger having ideas or leading people. Sometimes, (Ring)leaders find themselves miscast. Either they are former Idea Monkeys who were promoted in a position they don't particularly like, or they were put there because someone thought it was a good idea—and it wasn't. If you're a reluctant or unwilling (Ring)leader, it is time to ask for a new job.

Inventory your team to confirm who the strongest Idea Monkeys and (Ring)leaders are in your organization—you may be surprised. I like the quiz on page 2 a lot. But if you want something more scientific, you (Ring)leader you, try the Strengths Finder test at: http://www.strengthsfinder.com/113647/Homepage.aspx

Create an environment that champions ideas, leverages strengths, motivates minds, rewards risk-taking and organizes desired behavior. The easiest way to do that? Celebrate failure. Throw a party the next time someone swings for the fences—and misses.

Chapter 2

Meet the Idea Monkey

You need him, but he needs you as well.

When I told people I was considering using "Idea Monkey" as part of the title for this book, some of them immediately launched into their impression of Dieter from Saturday Night Live.

In the television sketch, Dieter is a bored German minimalist who interviews celebrities he has virtually no interest in and always brings the discussion around to his pet monkey, Klaus. News of my potential title always got people to utter a Dieter catch phrase: "Would you like to touch my monkey? Touch him! LOVE HIM!!"

I didn't mind because most comics (including the brilliant Mike Myers who created Dieter) are, in fact, Idea Monkeys. They will readily move from one thought to another, building on everyone else's ideas

"Would you like to touch my monkey?"

with the goal of creating a huge laugh. (Indeed, that is how Dieter came about. As the story goes, he is based on a bored waiter who once served Myers in a Toronto restaurant.) They won't stop until they reach their goal ... and you are busting a gut.

Stop for a second and think. Do you have a comedian at work who always has a joke and is quick to give you a new idea about virtually any topic? He's an Idea Monkey. This should be a good thing. What are you doing to harness that mind for good?

Professional comedians (who as we have seen are, by definition, Idea Monkeys) share the same gifts as the Idea Monkeys within your

Monkey Improv:

Listen to yourself. Idea Monkeys say "and" instead of "but" to help move ideas forward. You'll note that the same technique is used by improv comics.

organization. They understand that an idea is not an idea in reality until it moves beyond words to something that can be shared by many people. If all Myers did was say to himself, "You know, this awful waiter who has no interest in serving me could be the basis of a character," and then did nothing with the thought other than to tell a few friends about the bad meals, it would have been a waste of a perfectly bad dining experience.

Idea Monkeys share another common characteristic: they are incredibly curious. (My mother actually *did* call me Curious George as a kid.) This realization about curiosity became the key that led our company—Maddock Douglas—to make curiosity our primary hiring criteria. We literally screen for curiosity.

"Tell me about something you discovered today" is one of our standard interview questions. We aren't really looking for the discovery as much as the enthusiasm around it. Show me someone who can get sincerely excited about a new way to lace a shoe, and I will show you an Idea Monkey.

I have heard smart people say that if you want a happy culture, simply fire all the unhappy people. This sounds cold-hearted, but from experience I can tell you there is truth to it. Using the same logic, if you want an inventive culture, hire the curious people; start with Idea Monkeys. We do.

Ways to find the Monkey

- Count the "buts" vs. the "ands" in a conversation.
- Watch them navigate a website—do they wander or are they linear in their thinking?
- What's their Myers-Briggs type? Look for high "N" scores and lower "J" scores.
- Ask them to define an obscure word. Is this fun for them or frustrating?

Okay, we know Idea Monkeys are inventive, tenacious and curious. But this is supposed to be a business book. So why should you care? The answer is threefold:

1. **They are the driving force behind innovation.**

2. **They improve the quality of the workplace.** Simply put, ideas are the fuel for a growing company and a positive culture. The best people love to be working on huge, industry-altering projects in companies that are doing well. Many, like Mike Myers, will make you giggle as they help you see new possibilities.

3. **Wall Street absolutely loves Idea Monkeys.** How do we know? Wall Street regularly reports that the highest indicator of future profitability is a company's ability to consistently launch new products (one of the prime purviews of Idea Monkeys).

Let's take those three points one at a time.

THE AMOUNT OF A STOCK'S VALUE TIED TO THE FUTURE *

54%

* HARVARD BUSINESS REVIEW

THE DRIVING FORCE BEHIND INNOVATION

Our world is transformed every day by Idea Monkeys who drive innovation. A simple way to see their effect on an organization is to look at what happens to a company or industry after they arrive. Just Google Larry Page and Sergey Brin, Jack Welch at GE, Lou Gerstner at IBM, Reed Hastings at Netflix, Meg Whitman at eBay or Evan Williams at Twitter. If you want a classic case of the effect of monkey business, consider what happened when Steve Jobs left and later returned to Apple. Each of these leaders used business-brilliant ideas to change the way products and services go to market.

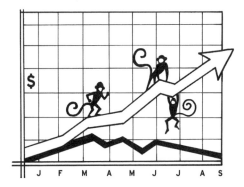

It's easy to think about creating change by altering business models, but you can drive innovation from any department. Phil Knight of Nike relied on branding to turn shoes into status symbols, and Peter Lynch of Fidelity used his beautiful financial mind to turn Magellan into one of the most sought after funds.

"Change before you have to."
– Jack Welch

IDEAS IDEAS IDEAS IDEAS

When P&G's then-chairman and CEO, A.G. Lafley, demanded that 50 percent of all new innovations come *through* R&D, not *from* R&D, he transformed P&G into the leader of what we now know as open innovation. It was as simple as redirecting his masterful scientists. He told them, "I know you are terrific at coming up with new ideas. Don't stop. But spend some of your time looking around to see what other interesting people are doing. Talk to them. Take them to lunch and let's see which of their ideas will work for us."

With that simple directive, he turned his scientists from being "just" a team of inventors to being a band of inventors/IP scouts/connectors.

It was a dramatic change. And one that has worked spectacularly. This revolutionary business model of *open* innovation has increased P&G's profitability and new product success and changed their culture. The feeling at P&G has gone from "if we didn't invent here, we are not interested," to "let's source the world and incorporate every wonderful idea we can find."

THE WORKPLACE GETS BETTER

Think about the last truly spectacular idea person that left your organization. Remember what they said when they left? If your experience is the same as mine, they said something like, "I have this really exciting opportunity to work on (widgets) that I just can't pass up." If you lead an innovative department or company, your job is to attract *and retain* Idea Monkeys because you will notice a meaningful difference the moment they are gone.

How do you keep them?

Research tells us that working on:

A. something meaningful,

B. in a lower stress environment,

C. with a reward system that makes sense, are all keys to attracting and retaining the best employees. These three criteria for A-Player employee attraction and retention are quite obviously linked through innovation. So being innovation-focused naturally drives a better culture while attracting and keeping brilliant, creative minds engaged. Here's how: successful innovation is intrinsically meaningful. Said differently, you have to be solving a significant need in order to have new product (or service) success. The happiest employees want to work on something meaningful. They naturally gravitate toward innovation assignments.

Personal Payoff

Innovation is typically on the radar of the CEO. So, to mix a metaphor, if you want to be under the spotlight, take on a major innovation initiative. It will bring out the best in you and get you immediately rewarded for performance.

You can smell a culture. Walk into any office and, in seconds, you will know whether something fun or insidious is cooking. That's why I am always thrilled when people say, "This feels like a really fun place to work," within the first few minutes of a tour. (The fact that they are taking the tour on a Segway might have something to do with it.)

Hmm... Innovation is the highest indicator of future profitability.

> "You know, I finally let that pain-in-the-butt, unhappy employee go and everyone seems so much happier."
> — every CEO I know

I am happy not just because they are right but because it is on purpose. We hire wonder-full people and let them work on really heady, world-changing projects. Respect, humility, challenge and talent are all key ingredients in the innovation stew. Not only does it smell good, it tastes great too.

THE IDEA MONKEY AND WALL STREET

The last business-related point has to do with how Idea Monkeys end up increasing a company's profits.

Ultimately, the reason companies in general, and marketers in particular, are interested in innovation is because of the money involved. And the smart money knows that relevant new products, services and business models are incredibly valuable for three key reasons. They:

- expand your customer base by attracting new clients.
- allow you to get a greater share of your customer's wallet. (The more products you offer that meet their needs, the more they will buy from you.)
- help retain existing customers. (They show you are actively listening to them by offering new things that meet their changing circumstances.)

Not surprisingly then, all these factors have an impact on the company and its share price.

Here is the way Gail McGovern, David Court, John Quelch and Blair Crawford put it in a *Harvard Business Review* article:

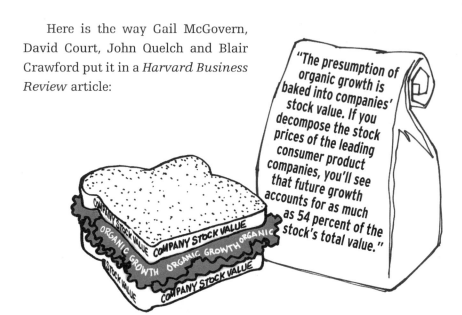

"The presumption of organic growth is baked into companies' stock value. If you decompose the stock prices of the leading consumer product companies, you'll see that future growth accounts for as much as 54 percent of the stock's total value."

That's an important point. When people discuss a company's share price, they love to talk about alliances and acquisitions as ways to get the stock price up. Both of those things are glamorous, but each is notoriously poor at generating greater shareholder value.

What *does* cause the share price to increase is a hot, original product. Think about what happens to Apple's shares every time it announces something new. (Can you say iPod and iPhone and iPad?) Is it any wonder then that many on Wall Street believe innovation is the leading indicator of future growth and profitability? There's even an index fund that just invests in what it thinks are the country's 20 most innovative companies.

And who makes all this innovation possible? Idea Monkeys. They are very valuable critters. Just ask the folks on Wall Street and their cousins, those who work in venture capital and private equity. Recently, they, too, have discovered the power of the Monkey. In the past, these companies followed the formula of:

Acquisition + Forced Efficiency = Profit

Professional investors would find companies that could benefit from operational expertise and put in their people to streamline everything. The combination of great management and cost cutting meant higher profits. But that strategy only works well if you are hoping to sell the company you acquired as soon as you wring out every bit of excess you can find.

If you want to grow the firm, you need a different strategy. Enter the Idea Monkey. Today, many VCs are actively looking for companies that have unique intellectual property that can be deployed in new, profitable ways. Professional money is now hiring chief marketing officers to invent new possibilities and launch new products and services based on the newly acquired IP. Why? Because they have learned that is the way to make a lot more money. While the cost-cutting savings are a one-time thing, the revenue created by Idea Monkeys can continue for a very long time.

Says Dustin Cohn, former director of marketing at Gatorade and now CMO of Optimer Brands, a financial holding company: "We actively pursue inventive marketers to help us reposition,

The Innovation Index

The list of firms that comprise the mutual fund compose the 25 most innovative companies, compiled by the aptly named Innovation Index Group, are updated once a year. For every company that is added, another drops out.

Not surprisingly, this index traditionally outperforms the returns turned in by the S&P 500 in most years. Here is a sampling of companies on the current list:

Amazon (AMZN)
Apple (AAPL)
BMW (BMW.GR)
Byd Co Ltd (1211.HK)
Coca-Cola (KO)
Fast Retailing (9983.JP)
Ford Motor Co (F)
General Electric (GE)
Google (GOOG)
Hewlett-Packard (HPQ)
Honda Motor Co (HMC)
Hyundai Motor Co (005380.KS)
IBM (IBM)
Intel (INTC)
LG Electronics (066570.KS)
Microsoft (MSFT)
Nintendo (NTDOY)
Nokia (NOK)
Procter & Gamble (PG)
Research in Motion (RIMM)
Samsung Electronics (005930.KS)
Sony (SNE)
Toyota Motor (TM)
Volkswagen AG (VOW.GR)
Walmart (WMT)

Each company's weight in the index is derived from a combination of two rankings. The first is a qualitative ranking based on the company's position in the annual Bloomberg Businessweek/BCG survey. The second is a quantitative ranking based on three factors used to estimate a company's innovation – three-year earnings growth, three-year sales growth and R&D as a percentage of sales. A composite score is calculated for each company by adding the qualitative and quantitative scores. For details, go to www.indices.standardandpoors.com.

reinvent and reinvigorate companies that we acquire. Ten years ago, my position didn't even exist in this industry. Today it is critical to our success."

I completely understand his point.

At our company, we believe that innovation is the *only* real source of *ongoing* competitive advantage. So this book could have just as easily been titled, "How to become an innovation power-house." (But frankly, talking about monkeys is way more fun.)

After delivering billions in new revenue through innovation, we can tell you that we absolutely agree with the folks on Wall Street: launching new products consistently is the domain of the Idea Monkey. When it comes to innovation, it really is a jungle out there. *(Sorry. Will someone please get Mike Myers on the phone? We need a real comedian.)*

So if you want to consistently dominate your industry, you need to know how to innovate. More specifically, you need to be able to release your inner Monkey and be an expert at managing the Monkeys on your team to help them become better innovators.

> **Warning: Monkeys love mixed metaphors**
> *(editors hate them)*

YOU NEED THE IDEA MONKEY

Later in this chapter, I am going to tell you about how my friend, Marc, helped save my business. But first let me talk about how a bunch of his friends helped save his, because it is the perfect example of why even the most talented executives need Idea Monkeys around them.

A bit about Marc: He is a brilliant operator. He founded and has grown a company that insures equipment—from nothing to a multimillion-dollar, midsized business. He's done it by selling through numerous sales channels—*builders, real estate agents, title companies, mortgage companies and directly to consumers*—and intimately knowing and refining every single metric that drives his business. This guy measures everything and therefore knows how to make small tweaks and get highly predictable (and profitable) results. He's the closest thing to an operational genius that I've seen. Marc is a (Ring)leader.

And he was stuck in a corner. The recession had driven the real estate industry—a primary sales channel—into the toilet. Like everyone else, Marc was surrounded by bad news. Insurance is a capital-intense business and he was worried that his firm could become undercapitalized, putting everything at risk.

Despite his amazing track record, he found himself tired, scared and out of ideas. Marc called his nine closest friends—businesspeople like himself—laid out his situation and asked for help. It was absolutely the right thing to do.

Dan Baker's excellent book titled *What Happy People Know* includes this very important lesson: you can't feel trapped and afraid and happy at the same time. One solution, according to Baker, is to manufacture choices. The more choices—even silly ones—you create, the less trapped you feel and the happier you can be.

Unfortunately, when you are feeling trapped, it is difficult to see or brainstorm choices. Marc needed choices. Marc needed ideas. And that is what his friends provided. Here are some of the questions that got Marc unstuck:

- What outcome do you want? What is standing in your way?
- What other services could you provide?
- If you were selling a product, what would it be?
- What would you do today if money did not matter?
- Have you considered_____? How about _____?
- Will you please come and work for me?

Marc left the meeting with nine pages of notes.

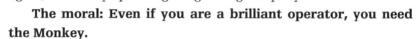

Three months later, Marc was negotiating the acquisition of two companies while turning down hefty purchase offers from a VC and a competitor. He was predicting (correctly) a record year and was himself again, brilliantly operating his growing company.

The moral: Even if you are a brilliant operator, you need the Monkey.

In fact, there is no professional practice, no personality type and no department that can't be helped by the myriad of choices generated by great Idea Monkeys, which is another reason companies that are leading innovators consistently find, place and grow Idea Monkeys in every department. And it is almost always the Monkey who pushes these departments and practices into fame through the conceptualization and actualization of new ideas. Don't believe me?

Financial skeptics, please look up **Peter Drucker.**

"Knowledge has to be improved, challenged and increased constantly or it vanishes." –Peter Drucker

IT skeptics, may I introduce you to **Bill Gates?**
"If I had some set idea of a finish line, don't you think I would have crossed it years ago?" –Bill Gates

Marketing skeptics, I give you **Alex Bogusky.**
"Fear is the mortal enemy of innovation, creativity and happiness." –Alex Bogusky

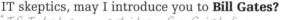

Operational skeptics, please look into **Henry Ford.**
"Enthusiasm is the sparkle in your eyes, the swing in your gait. The grip of your hand, the irresistable surge of will and energy to execute your ideas." –Henry Ford

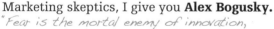

Business model skeptics, check out **Doris K. Christopher.**
"We provide people with ways to be creative in the kitchen by giving them simple, fast ideas and the tools to accomplish them." –Doris K. Christopher

You get the idea. The Monkey's gifts are not, and should not be, limited to the marketing department, although that's where the uninspired often think they should live.

HELPING THE MONKEY

Spend enough time around innovation and you become aware of a startling analogy: ideas are just like children. Ideas need a loving set of parents to conceive them, encourage them, challenge them and protect them until they are ready to stand on their own. Born as simple insights, good parenting will produce products, services and business models that literally change the world.

My experience is that all Monkeys find great joy in conceiving an idea, but only the most practiced know how to expertly actualize their ideas. Just like ideas need parents to guide them, so too do Monkeys need help guiding the best ideas to market.

Unfortunately, because of departmental silos, most innovation processes use multiple sets of foster parents instead of a dedicated set of idea parents. So, what started out as an innocent insight with nothing but potential winds up being a weak idea that never becomes what it could have been: brilliant.

Enter the Idea Monkeys. The Monkey's role is to have the idea *and* to become—or inspire—the key parenting figure(s) that will drive the best ideas into existence.

How? The best companies establish a small core innovation team—made up of all the key departments necessary to take a product from idea to marketplace (so yes, finance and manufacturing people are members)—that stays with the insight all the way from discovery to launch.

This team approach works for three reasons: it is small, it is focused and it is empowered. The leadership of the company has created clear objectives like:

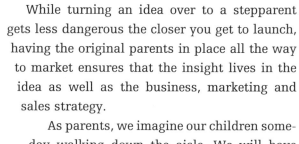

- You will bring us (three) ideas that we can launch in 12 months.
- These ideas can be a product, service or business model as long as they deliver the incremental dollars.
- These ideas will live under brand X.
- Each idea will deliver X million in incremental dollars.

The team is powerful: it has a budget, complete authority to make the project happen and unlimited access to any part of the organization—including the executive leadership team. (Note that while this type of parenting team may resemble internal teams that have lived in your organization in the past, those teams most likely were not given the direction and lacked the authority of the ones outlined above. Most importantly, they probably were disbanded long before the idea hit the market.)

While turning an idea over to a stepparent gets less dangerous the closer you get to launch, having the original parents in place all the way to market ensures that the insight lives in the idea as well as the business, marketing and sales strategy.

As parents, we imagine our children someday walking down the aisle. We will have been there for them every step of the way. We will have done everything that we could to encourage, protect and challenge them to be the best they could be. And when they are successful, we'll know that we've had more than a little to do with it.

Ideas are just like our kids. They deserve good parenting.

THE MONKEY'S WHY

In his pivotal work, *Man's Search for Meaning,* Victor E. Frankl talks about his experience of living through Nazi concentration camps.

As a trained psychologist, Frankl eventually was somehow able to accept his horrifying experience as an opportunity to "add deeper meaning to my life."

Even under such incredibly inhuman conditions, he saw himself driven by a higher purpose. When speaking about this ability, Frankl references Nietzsche's words, "He who has a why to live for can bear with almost any how." Frankl was in touch with his why and it literally saved his life.

Simon Sinek, a friend, company owner and consultant, helps people and companies find their "why." He argues that average companies know their what: "we sell computers." Good companies know their how: "we configure computers to your specifications." But great companies are all about their why: "We will change the world with beautiful technology."

I've already told you that Idea Monkey's are tenacious idea promoters. Now their secret: creating ideas is their "why."

The Care and Feeding of Your Monkey:

TIP: If you have lost – or fear you are losing – your inner-Monkeyness, here's a suggestion: do your best to think like a four-year-old. Observe and be grateful for all the wonders around you. There is a reason that kids can stare at a blade of grass and giggle at the sound of a fly hitting a window. If you want your life to be rich with curiosity, gratefulness and sense of wonder, you need to keep your inner Idea Monkey alive. One way to do that is to see the world as kids do.

You're right... Monkeys don't really eat carrots

80% OF NEW ENTREPRENEURS ARE OPTIMISTIC — (Despite the fact that 66% of new businesses fail in the first 4 years.)

THE BIRTH OF AGENCY OF INNOVATION® SERVICES

Our firm is an Innovation Agency. We pretty much made up this category when the Monkeys running our company recognized that the industry we had started in (marketing) was a weak platform for inventing new things. Our ideas, our "kids," were not making it out in the real world. While our competitors were bitching about "the good old days" (they still are), we created a new type of business model and process to address our client's need for a single set of "parents" to help insights turn into industry-changing ideas.

We've created a company devoted to the mission of driving industry-changing ideas to market. We now have parenting teams managing a proven process that efficiently discovers needs; brainstorms products, services and business models to meet those needs; brands the best ideas; and launches them into market. We've helped make (literally) billions of dollars for clients like McDonald's, Allstate, CNH, SCJ and GE. We've enabled the brilliance of Idea Monkeys through a process and business model that moves from insights into new products.

So our real business is finding Monkeys, managing Monkeys and coupling them with activators and process. (I'd call it "Monkey business," but that would be annoyingly predictable.)

THE MONKEY NEEDS YOU AS WELL

As much as you need the Idea Monkey, that's how much the Monkey needs you. The Monkey cannot act alone. He needs actualizers in every department to take what might be just a raw thought and form it into something that is executable. He needs a yin for his yang. He needs (Ring)leaders. I learned that lesson the hard way.

In June of 2004, my good friend and fellow business owner, Marc, called and said, "Mike, we've known each other for years, and you don't seem well. You're clearly under a lot of stress and you're not yourself. I don't know if it's me who can help you, but maybe I can. Just name the time and I'll be there for you. Even if you don't want to meet, I think it's time you got some outside perspective."

I knew Marc was right. I was a mess. Six months earlier, we'd lost 37 percent of our business when two of our largest clients left us inside of 30 days because of a sale and change in strategy. (One was Verizon. We were helping them put new phone technology in airplanes, but 9/11 helped push them out of that game.) While most people would view losing 37 percent of their revenue as a signal to dramatically cut costs, yours truly saw it as a signal to rally the troops. "We can overcome this! We will sell our way out of this hole!"

Six months later, this unfortunate spasm of inspired leadership had led us to burn through about $1.3 million in cash. I was exhausted, defeated and felt absolutely trapped by the circumstances that I'd helped orchestrate. And for the very first time in my life, I was completely out of ideas. I had lost my Monkeyness.

If that wasn't bad enough, there were personnel issues. As a company, we'd reached the point where we needed to fully embrace innovation as our future, moving dramatically away from our marketing roots. Unfortunately, only about half of the company was committed to this vision or were a talent fit for the model, which meant we needed new leadership from the top down. People were going to lose their jobs. The prospect of saying goodbye to my friends was tearing me up.

I thought I was handling it well, but obviously I wasn't. One day I came home and there was a letter—a prayer actually—from my 7-year-old son. He was asking God to help me stop worrying. My wife begged me to go see a doctor because I couldn't sleep for more than three hours without waking up in a panic. What happened to the happy-go-lucky, anything-is-possible Idea Monkey?

I know now that what happened is a classic example of what occurs when a company becomes out of balance. In Chapter 12 we'll talk about the absolutely critical partnerships that create a yin for the Monkey's yang. For now, let's just say that the Monkey was running the ship by himself and the ship was sinking. (How's that for an odd pairing of images?)

Looking back, I know that Marc's call probably saved our business. I had reached my breaking point and, not surprisingly, so had our company. The very evening of Marc's call, I sat surrounded by Marc and eight

EVOLUTION   REVOLUTION

of my closest business friends. Thankfully, they recognized both the symptoms and the cause of our challenges. During our four-hour meeting, they were able to reactivate the ideator and refocus my energies on strategies that would get me and our company back in balance.

Man does six months make a difference! First, on the advice of my advisors, I took four weeks off to get rested, regain perspective and refocus. When I came back we:

- started a completely new, separate company led by three MD employees who wanted to keep doing what our "old agency" did. (This firm, McGuffin Creative Group, is thriving today.)

- (those who remained) fully embraced a new positioning as an innovation agency and helped me outline the processes and staff needed to get us there.
- found a new president, Raphael Louis Vitón, a passionate master of operations, and a leader who was a complete yin for my yang.
- set in place a strategy that has led us to quadruple the size of our firm in six years.

Most importantly, my wife, kids and teammates will tell you that I was myself again and the options were limitless.

What was the lesson I learned?

I had ideated myself and our company into the proverbial corner. We had become a company of undisciplined ideas—when one business concept did not work, we simply came up with another. I had failed to realize that my type of energy, madness, talent or whatever you want to call it was dangerous if not balanced with a disciplined partner, process and people.

Great companies and great leaders recognize the need for Idea Monkeys to drive innovation. But they also know the importance of management, guidance and practices to keep the best thinkers and ideas on course.

We will talk about how to channel your Monkey next.

This space intentionally left empty so you can doodle.

QUICK! HAVE AN IDEA AND JOT IT DOWN HERE.

> _____
_____
_____

> _____
_____
_____

> _____
_____
_____

> _____
_____
_____

> _____
_____
_____

(RING)LEADER To-Dos

Practice spotting the tell-tale signs and words of an Idea Monkey. If you constantly hear someone say, "We could do this, this and this," or "building on Susie's idea," or "would be incredibly cool to do ... " you have an Idea Monkey on your hands.

Be direct and deliberate about planning for a symbiotic/synergistic relationship with the Idea Monkey. Tell them you love their energy, passion and ideas, and your job is to channel them and make them more effective (and you would love their help in doing so).

Get comfortable with leading from outside of your comfort zone by experimenting with the Idea Monkey in a variety of problem-solving opportunities. Fight the idea of reining them in. Take chances. Have fun.

Continuously gauge your appreciation for the Monkey's strengths—yes, they can be an absolute pain in the butt—and focus on channeling their effectiveness when working together.

Create safety nets of continuity for idea parenting vs. less-invested hand-offs. In other words, keep teams together as long as possible through the process of moving ideas to market.

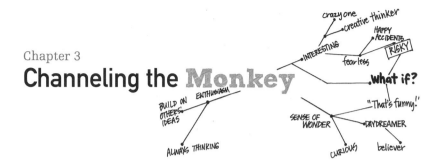

Chapter 3

Channeling the Monkey

It is Monday morning, first thing, and the phone
rings. It's an old friend and she's excited. She jumps
right in, "I have an idea that I think is really big.
Can you meet me for coffee to talk about it?"

We meet for coffee, and guess what? It really *is* a big idea. It is
potentially a giant, life-changing idea.

My reaction? (And I mean this with sincere respect for my buddy.)
Big whippitty, skippitty doo. (Here's a hint: a storage company could
potentially make millions with this idea.)

Please don't interpret my reaction as cynical. I've just come to
understand that there is a common misperception about success
related to creative invention. The thinking goes something like this:
all you need to do (especially in America) is come up with one, really
big idea and you are on easy street for the rest of your life. My experience is that this is simply not true. In fact, for many (read: "Idea
Monkeys"), coming up with ideas is really easy. Executing a successful idea? Well, that's a different story. For the people who come up
with ideas, this is often the toughest thing of all.

Stop and think for a moment. Don't you have a really **big idea** that
you have been sitting on for a number of years? Perhaps it is a gadget
that makes cleaning an aquarium easier, or a software program that
will revolutionize the way youth soccer is managed, or a simple way
for airlines to speed up boarding, or.... If you are like most, you had

the idea some time ago, and *some day*, you are going to do something with it.

You are not alone, my partner in procrastination. Most everyone is guilty of this—even people who own and run innovation agencies.

Speaking nonmetaphorically, I am a fisherman. Like most fishermen, I dream of coming up with the next great fishing lure. I carry around hundreds of different types of lures because I never want to be caught without the latest, greatest super bait. When it comes to fishing, I am "always prepared" and I just assume every other former Boy Scout fisherman must behave the same way.

About ten years ago on a freezing morning in the middle of Canada, I noticed an annoying challenge with jigs. (Note to nonobsessed, nonfishermen: a jig is a simple, usually colored, weight with a hook sticking out the back. You can add live bait or plastic worms to the jig—whatever your fancy.)

Any fisherman who has used a jig has picked up one with the line hole, the place where you attach your hook, completely painted

"jig"

shut. It isn't surprising. The jigs are mass produced and painted the same way, so it isn't a shock that some would make their way into stores with the hole where the hook is supposed to go painted over.

On that freezing cold morning in Canada, I saw it as a huge problem waiting for an invention. And so the EyeOpener™ was born. This crafty little invention promised to save thousands of ex-Boy Scout fishermen around the world hundreds of hours by popping the paint right out of the eye of the jig.

"jig"

eye

I talked about it and I talked about it. I took friends to coffee and asked if they thought it was a really big idea. I protected the name, I drew up the mechanicals ... and then I didn't do a darn thing with it. Work, family and other more promising ideas took precedence. It wasn't exactly that I had abandoned it. I would get around to it—someday.

Hmm... **70,000**

That is the number of thoughts the human brain produces on an average day.

I still remember my wife starting to cry in a Walmart in Iowa when she saw *my* idea being marketed by someone else. She had no idea that I had dozens of similar, even bigger "big ideas" in a drawer back home.

Like I said, ideas are easy. Execution? Not so much.

Today when I hear an executive tell me they need a new "big idea," I assure them that they are mistaken. They have people with drawers full of big ideas. They likely have a few themselves. Most leaders don't need ideas, they need to understand how to execute their best ideas and, more importantly, channel the Idea Monkeys who have the potential to help bring the best ideas to market.

HOW COME WE DON'T DO ANYTHING WITH ALL THOSE IDEAS?

So what stops people from bringing industry-changing ideas to market? After seeing this "I've-got-a-big-idea-that-I-am-really-not-going-to-do-anything-with" trend for many years, I believe people freeze because they secretly fear failure. Perhaps they believe there is more to innovation success than simply coming up with the big idea. *Newsflash:* they're correct.

So, in an effort to better humanity (and keep you from seeing your spouse cry in a Walmart in Iowa), I offer you the simple formula that will consistently and systematically help you lead more industry-changing ideas to market. (Imagine the friends and fame you are about to attain. I'd uncork some champagne immediately.)

There are three ingredients to successful innovation.

First, there must be a need or an insight. What problem does this idea solve? Is the problem important enough and big enough to elicit action and result in the required amount of cash flow? Have you identified the precise needs you're fulfilling? Often a new product or service can fill many needs. You want to focus on the precise (biggest, most pressing) one.

Next (not first), you need the idea. What product, service or business model fixes the problem in an efficient, novel and proprietary way? You're likely not the first person to notice this challenge. How have existing ideas failed to hit the mark?

Finally, once you have the insight and idea, it is time to create the communication that connects the insight with your idea.

Remember, a great idea poorly communicated is as ineffective as a lousy idea brilliantly communicated.

You have a BIG idea. great.

answer me
these
questions three:

1.) is there a need?
does it solve a problem?

2) what IS the idea?
product, service, bidness
model

3) How are you going to
tell the world about
your solution?

The wheel was not man's first innovation. Several significant inventions predated the wheel by

THE INNOVATION FORMULA: SHORT VERSION

So to change the world, you need to create the synchronized intersection—the tiny shaded area within the three circles below—of the need (insight), the idea (product, service or business model) and the communication that connects the two.

This simple formula is easy to describe, but perilously difficult to achieve. Turns out that ideas are easy, insights are easy and communication is easy. Getting them all to work in unison? For most, really, really hard ... *this* is why most new products fail.

To use another metaphor, think of the circle diagram as a three-legged stool. Without one leg,

the stool falls, and so, too, will your innovation initiative. You may have a great team of brilliant idea people/Monkeys, but unless you can get them to understand this simple concept, they will fail. Your job as the Lord of the Innovation Jungle is to make them understand. Now, thump your Tarzan chest because you just learned something really important.

thousands of years: sewing needles, woven cloth, rope, basket weaving, boats and even the flute.

FAILURE 101

Examples of not understanding the innovation formula (and subsequent failures) are everywhere. A classic example of this concept is TIVO. By now you know what a DVR does, but when TIVO launched in the 1990s, nobody did.

TIVO filled a general need: people were busy and they simply could not stop their lives to watch their favorite TV show. TIVO had an amazing technology (an idea) that would solve this problem: digital video recording—your favorite shows captured while you carried on with your life.

But since they were apparently not sure exactly how people thought about lack of time, they were apparently unclear which of the bevy of juicy benefits to talk about. You see, TIVO knew that they not only helped you save time, they also:

- Found and recorded your favorite shows
- Allowed you to transfer these shows to VCR tapes
- Let you play your shows in slow motion or frame-by-frame
- Could suggest shows you should be watching
- Could let you watch live TV while it recorded up to two other different shows
- Would help you record in high def, low def, mid def ...
- Could help you fly ... kidding, but by this point you'd think it should be able to

In hindsight, I am pretty sure that the most relevant benefit of TIVO at the time was that it was ten times easier to use than a VCR— no switching tapes, no full tapes, no tapes at all. But because TIVO did not know the primary need they were fulfilling, they told people about a myriad of features and functions that left many confused and frozen in their VCR world.

TIVO provides you with a big watchout related to the formula for innovation success: *Fail to identify and communicate a single burning consumer need/solution and your product will likely fail.* For years, TIVO struggled to woo the masses because they failed to connect the idea to a need. (And because they couldn't do that, there was no way to create any kind of compelling message.)

Meanwhile, anyone who tried TIVO became a raging fan because the technology was so incredibly transformational.

Thankfully, the raging fans and millions of marketing dollars eventually saved TIVO. But seriously, do you want your life to be this difficult? I think not.

INDUSTRIES IN NEED OF SERIOUS MONKEY CHANNELING

What if I told you insurance is one of the most innovative industries I know? (Hold the smirks. I'm serious.)

What if I went further and said that insurance companies were poised to assume the leadership position when it comes to creating new products, services and business models in our economy? You'd probably think I was trying to sell you a whole life policy. (As opposed to a half life policy?)

Well, the fact that you don't believe me—and again I am being totally sincere—says a lot about the problem insurance companies and many other conservative, risk-averse industries have when it comes to innovation. Perhaps this is a problem that your industry may have as well, and therein lies a tale.

Insurance companies are living proof that if you don't have all three parts of the innovation formula, the results are guaranteed to be suboptimal.

As you just read, innovation occurs when:

1. there is a significant need or insight.
2. a product, service or business model meets that need.
3. there is clear communication that connects No. 1 to No. 2.

By this definition, the insurance industry is clearly innovative— at least when it comes to creating a product that fulfills a need. Consider some of the more obvious benefits available through one type of coverage: life insurance.

LIFE INSURANCE

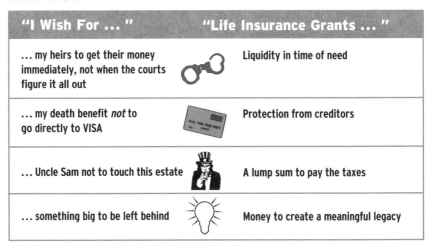

"I Wish For ... "		"Life Insurance Grants ... "
... my heirs to get their money immediately, not when the courts figure it all out		Liquidity in time of need
... my death benefit *not* to go directly to VISA		Protection from creditors
... Uncle Sam not to touch this estate		A lump sum to pay the taxes
... something big to be left behind		Money to create a meaningful legacy

But this table begs one obvious question: did you know about these benefits? Probably not. Insurance products often have the need and the idea. What is missing is the ability to communicate their ideas in a way that is relevant to increasingly busy people.

Insurance is not the only industry with this opportunity. Virtually every industry falls into the trap of communicating using language that only insiders understand. Once these industries figure out a better way to communicate—and if they read Chapter 4 they will know how—they will be able to leverage all of the tools at their disposal.

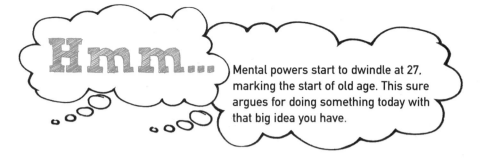

Mental powers start to dwindle at 27, marking the start of old age. This sure argues for doing something today with that big idea you have.

YOU ARE NOW FRUSTRATED AND CONSIDERING PUTTING DOWN THE BOOK. PLEASE DON'T.

Many leaders become frustrated at this point because they have been trained to believe that big ideas are readily apparent, so when they can't figure out precisely what is wrong with their innovation engine—"why isn't the world beating a path to our door?"—they throw up their hands in disgust.

Thank you, God, this is usually about the time people call Maddock Douglas. So we have the benefit of hearing about the symptoms of innovation dysfunction when leaders like you are most frustrated. Chances are, you will find some of the following extremely familiar. (We'll go into this in much greater detail—going step-by-step—in the second half of the book. But for now, let's just hit the highlights.)

SIGNS OF INNOVATION DYSFUNCTION (PREPARE TO HEAR YOURSELF WHINE)

1. The Challenge: No big ideas

The way the complaint is usually presented: "We've been innovating for years and have hit the wall. What we're really looking for are a couple of revolutionary ideas for our incredibly mature category."

Solution: Revolutionary ideas most often come from outside your category. Therefore, you must look at parallel industries and rely heavily on thinkers who don't walk your halls every day (see Chapter 4).

Extra Credit: Are you really looking for revolutionary ideas? Really and truly? Or are you just saying it because that's what leaders are supposed to say? If you really (truly) mean it, you won't accept business as usual.

Be aware!

Each department will perceive needs relative to its own expertise and experience. We recommend doing quantitative work to test insight platforms *before* ideation.

Most will tell you that this limits big thinking, because applying the filter of data early on naturally eliminates some options.

Wrong. This simply assures that all of the new ideas align with the most important customer needs—you want people brainstorming in the right sandbox.

2. The Challenge: Too many ideas.

The way the complaint is usually presented: "We have hundreds of ideas. We need help figuring out which are the really big ideas."

Solution: Congratulations on recognizing what many leaders overlook in the zeal to make a mark.

But know this: you don't have hundreds of good ideas. You likely have about ten—but which ten? Sit with the key influencer in each division of the company—the ones who you need to have on board to make things happen—and have them list each criteria they require to rate an idea "excellent."

Sample Criteria might include:

- In market in 18 months
- $50 million in incremental sales
- We can actually manufacture it

Now, go back and use these criteria and rank every concept you have. Take the winners through a formal innovation process.

3. The Challenge: "We know too much."

The way the complaint is usually presented: "We know our customer better than anyone. But we're unsure which of their needs to address first."

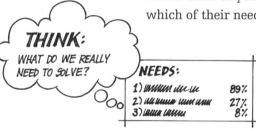

Solution: Want to bet? When was the last time you did extensive voice of the customer work? We've never (never, ever, ever ...) presented qualitative video clips without senior management being shocked at what their consumer/customer—who "we know so well"—was saying about their company.

Where there is real understanding about the consumer, there is true possibility for innovation. Where there is a big insight, you can create a big innovation.

Extra Credit: And who are you listening to?

For example, look at what is happening with tweens. It used to be that moms made most of the buying decisions. Today, armed with smart phones and the Internet, kids have much more to say about what gets purchased.

4. The Challenge: We're getting our asses kicked. (And we can't get out of our own way.) This may be due to politics, apathy or even lack of talent.

The way the complaint is usually presented: The only people who say this are senior managers (and we *only* hear it after we have been out to dinner with them, and they have had a couple of drinks). Then they say, "We're sick of our competitors successfully launching ideas that we had in our pipeline years ago."

Solution: The best innovators have a system in which they rotate innovation teams (Idea Monkeys) to get fresh eyes on old ideas. These new innovation leaders are often required to test old ideas along with their new ones.

Extra Credit: Too often ideas favored by the boss get undo consideration. (Hey boss, I know that innovation is fun, but unless you are willing to be a good Monkey and play by your own rules, hands off!) All concepts must meet the prescribed innovation criteria, all must address a quantified need, and all must live on only if the consumer says so.

5. The problem: We must be ahead of our time.

The way the complaint is usually presented: "We know we have discovered the right insight and have a brilliant technology to meet the need, but our customers don't seem excited enough about it."

Solution: Research is more than just a way to uncover and validate needs; it is a way to hear how your customers talk about them. Take care to create an innovation team that includes the writers and creative folk who will have to manage the launch of the idea—no troop is complete without them. They will make sure they use your customer's own language as they creatively describe the idea—so they recognize it.

Extra Credit: As the TIVO example proves, resist the urge to talk about more than one benefit. Just because your product can deliver multiple benefits doesn't mean you have to talk about every one of them. Thrill your customer by delivering on the primary benefit brilliantly, and allow them to discover the others on their own.

A QUICK REVIEW

In the context of our formula for successful innovation:

Need + Idea + Communication = A Winner

you can see how creating new products becomes substantially easier.

> Idea Monkeys are passionately focused on pushing their ideas into the market. Your job as the "(Ring)leader" is to help channel them with simple questions and practices that assure they are staying true to the innovation formula and thus increase their chances of market acceptance (i.e., success).

That sounds simple. But you know from past experience, it is not. To help you keep the Idea Monkey on track, you might want to follow a script that sounds something like this the next time the Monkey comes up with "something totally great."

Idea Monkey: "I have an idea."

(Ring)leader: "Terrific. Show me the need it is fulfilling and how you know that the need is significant. If you aren't ready for that, I can help you map out some efficient research to verify the need."

Idea Monkey: "We're going to have a brainstorming session. Want to come and participate?"

(Ring)leader: "Sure, but before I do, tell me about the one or two needs we'll be brainstorming to solve. Also, we don't want to be spending too much time on old thinking, so what outside resources have you invited to brainstorm with us?"

Idea Monkey: "We've come up with about 15 different things our customers want us to fix."

(Ring)leader: "Terrific! Let's do some research to figure out the top two areas of need and how our customers talk about them. Then you and your experts can start coming up with ideas to solve them!"

Idea Monkey: "We have the idea, and here's the good news. It has way more functionality than any of our competitors' products. It is unbelievably cool!"

(Ring)leader: "Awesome. About which function is our customer most excited? How are they talking about it? Let's make sure we use their words—not ours—in stressing the function they like best."

WHO CHANNELS YOUR MONKEY?

There is a famous story about Roy and Walt Disney. Walt, once again, had gotten incredibly excited about an idea that he'd been thinking about and had made an enthusiastic presentation to his brother, Roy, who ran operations. Roy's response was that Walt's idea was going to cost more than $1 million to execute, to which Walt responded, "Roy, why do you bother me with these meaningless details?"

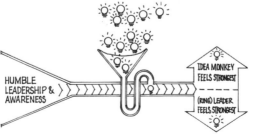

I mentioned earlier that the Idea Monkey can become a destructive distraction. This is particularly true when the Monkey is a leader in the organization. Without Roy, Walt would have admittedly been just another dreamer. But Walt recognized his weakness as well as his strengths. He had Roy to help him focus on the best ideas and, more importantly, take care of the incredibly hard work of implementing them. The same is true for Roy. Without Walt, he was an operational expert. With Walt, he was able to help make millions of children smile—and shareholders rich.

This pattern is consistently seen with famous Idea Monkeys even if you are not aware of the sometimes quiet partnership. The ideator and the activator:

- Rodgers and Hammerstein
- Jobs and Wosniak
- Orville and Wilbur
- MJ and Phil Jackson
- Elvis and the Colonel ... ok, you get the idea.

Because this idea is so important, I am going to give it its own chapter, Chapter 12 "Discovering a Yin to Your Yang or Are You a Walt Disney or a Roy Disney?" But for now, let me finish the thought with this.

I love Marcus Buckingham's language in his book *Now, Discover Your Strengths.* His premise is, first find out what "makes you feel strong" and then align all your activities against these strengths. So, you need to begin by asking what makes you feel strong? Looking at the three components of our innovation formula is a great place to start. Are you about ideas, insights or connecting the two with inspired communication?

Great leaders understand their strengths and weaknesses. They make it a point to find partners whose strengths complement their weaknesses. Do you know yours? The proof should not be in the revelation, rather in the complementary partnerships you have formed. If you lead departments or companies, it should be evident in the way you hire, fire, matchmake and coach.

By the end of this book, my goal is to make you feel comfortable freeing the Idea Monkey inside you as well as channeling your ideas and the ideas of your troops.

Now, let's dig a bit deeper into the most important traits and practices of our favorite Idea Monkeys and their brilliant operating partners. Let's see how what they have learned can benefit you.

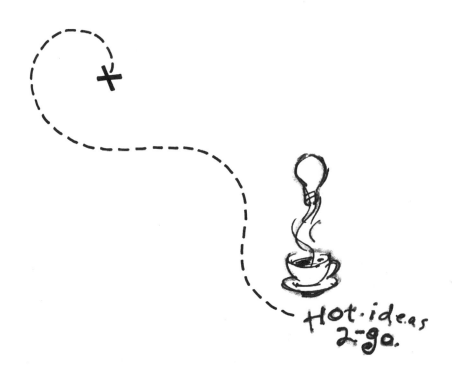

Hot·ideas
2-go.

WRITE FIVE AMUSINGLY TRUE THINGS PEOPLE SAY ABOUT YOUR INDUSTRY BEHIND YOUR BACK.

> _____

> _____

> _____

> _____

> _____

(RING)LEADER To-Dos

Keep the Idea Monkey's energy focused on the synchronized intersection of the need, the idea and the communication that connects the two (hint: it's the equivalent of an idea generation trifecta—Monkeys love that).

Clearly define, quantify and prioritize primary needs (not just any needs) for the Monkey to sink his teeth into—that way his ideas will start out closer to the "finish line."

Further focus the Idea Monkey's efforts with clear, prioritized objectives and success criteria that serve as idea guardrails.

Be humble. If you don't like an idea, identify which part has you stuck with an "I wish" statement (e.g., I wish I could figure out how to get that idea through legal).

Create new expectations and shared rewards for both Monkeys and (Ring)leaders—subtly underscoring that Monkeys need to work and play well with others.

(Your brilliant, insightful, amusing,
life-changing notes go here.
Also useful for wrapping small fish.)

Chapter 4
Inside Out and Outside In-novation
The Delicate Dance of Innovation

There is a great saying in the South:

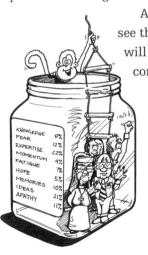

"You can't read the label when you are sitting inside the jar."

This applies directly to your ability to innovate. If you have been with a company for more than six months, it is time you realize: You're stuck in the jar. The way you think about new ideas is distorted by the corporate container you find yourself working within.

As a result, it is extremely difficult for you to see the priceless ideas all around you—ideas that will become the new products and services your competitor will use to steal market share.

I know, I know. I can't be talking about you. I had the same reaction initially. But if any of the following sounds familiar, you are in the jar—just like I was.

KNOWLEDGE 8%
FEAR 12%
EXPERTISE 22%
MOMENTUM 4%
FATIGUE 7%
HOPE 5%
MEMORIES 10%
IDEAS 21%
APATHY 11%

SYMPTOMS OF BEING IN THE JAR

You know you are in the jar when you hear the following:

"We've tested that idea. It didn't work." What idea exactly? People who are in the jar interpret ideas based on how they last saw them. When they hear about a scooter, they think skateboard, not Segway. When someone says "auction," they think Sotheby's, not eBay. They've literally judged the idea before it has been re-envisioned. Their experience blinds them to the possibilities of the future.

Silence. When your team is trying to brainstorm new ideas, the room gets eerily quiet. The reality is that they are probably desperately trying to be creative, but they keep seeing hurdles. They don't want to appear negative, so they decide to be silent and nod a lot.

"Yes, but ... " Trying to be polite, people will just "but" other people's ideas to death. ("It is a really interesting idea you are proposing, but it will never work because ... ") This is usually not about intent—they really want to be helpful—but they are too busy thinking about regulatory issues, manufacturing issues, political issues, budgetary issues ... deadening their ability to be creative. Not only are they in the jar, but the lid is really tight.

An idea for (yet another) safe line extension.

Line extensions and evolutionary innovation should be a part of your plan. But when that's all your team is producing, it probably means they have lost the ability to recognize big ideas, or worse, they no longer have the fortitude to push the rope up the hill, given all the resistance they have faced in the past.

"Huh?" If you are often asked by smart consultants or newcomers to your company what in God's name you are talking about, you're probably in the jar. Seems that after a few months in the jar together, we develop our own language. Often laced with industry-borne acronyms, this strange way of communicating seeps into our customer and client communications.

A few years back, we scored big points with about 40 million customers when we convinced a client to change the last line on its monthly billing statement from "Account Balance," the way the idea was referred to inside the company, to "What you owe," the phrase most of us use when we talk about our debts.

You are surrounded by hundreds of similar examples.

Ever notice how a five-year-old can walk into a situation and ask an innocent question that elicits the "because that's the way we do it" response? Then you realize you've never really questioned why you do it that way? Five-year-olds are too young to be in the jar.

So are you.

GET GREAT IDEAS FLOWING WITH A JOB SWAP

I went to high school with hundreds of kids in each grade, which made physical education a circus. But a technique that my gym teachers used is a great model for how to infuse energy into your team while generating powerful, new ideas at the same time.

Here's what they did. The teachers could not possibly create a game a hundred kids could play, so they divided the gym into quadrants and set up four games that were all coached by a different instructor. At the beginning of class, each coach would describe his game, the challenge and the rules. Then each kid was assigned to a game. In one corner, kids would be playing kickball, and in another volleyball—you get the idea.

After 15 minutes or so, a whistle would blow and the head coach would yell, "Rotate!" which would be the signal for each group to go to the next game. We all got to play four different games, which kept the class interesting, taught us new skills and it allowed kids to show off their different talents.

This same, simple technique will work wonders inside your company. Formalizing ways for different departments and work teams to "rotate" to focus on different challenges will create renewed energy and result in big, new ideas.

Coming up with as many ideas as possible is good, but not all ideas are created equal.

How do you go about screening them? Here is the best initial, best sorting device we know.

Ask, does the idea:
1. identify a significant need or insight?
2. naturally lead to the creation of a product, service or business model that meets that need?
3. have clear communication that connects No. 1 to No. 2?

Insight/ Need

COM- mercialization
COM- munication

Idea: product, service or business model

Here are three ways it could work:

1. **Junior to Senior.** Grab a very junior person in your company. The perfect candidate is someone smart, creative, brave—and too naïve to worry about failing. Take your toughest challenge and ask your junior associate to generate as many ideas and questions about the challenge as possible. Tell them they are going to get points for quality *and* quantity.

While they are working on their project for you, work on their toughest challenge.

Give yourself a few hours and then get together to discuss your ideas. You may be surprised at how much you both learn.

2. **Department Switch.** Try the same exercise as above with people from opposite departments. It's amazing how much you will learn watching the folks from operations handle the biggest marketing challenges and vice versa. For example, the operations people will appreciate the many ways a problem may be solved—they often feel as though they have already determined best practices—while the marketing people are often stunned at how much more efficiently they could be accomplishing their goals.

3. **Boss/Industry Swap.** Here's the best one of all: switch leadership roles. Doing this inside your company will produce similar results, but with more fireworks because of the bigger egos involved. And if you want to have a whole bunch of fun and learn way more, find a company in an unrelated industry and do a job swap. What would a senior marketer from retail see in your manufacturing company?

So, the next time you feel a lack of energy or ideas within your teams, yell "Rotate!" and watch the magic happen.

REALLY IMPORTANT: The order here matters. Start with the Insight, then have an Idea.

A white guy, a white guy and a white guy walk into a bar … did I lose you yet?

Thought so. Nothing interesting was going to come from that joke. Humor works when you have an unexpected, compelling outcome. So  does the innovation process, and it's often achieved by adding diversity—getting the ideas from people of different ages, genders, races and ethnic backgrounds—people with varying perspectives, personalities, experiences, mind-sets, etc.

But when most think about the topic of diversity, it is invariably in terms of "inclusion," "multicultural acceptance." That has tremendous merit, but why the heck when you hear the word "diversity" are you suddenly thinking like someone who has Equal Employment Opportunity responsibilities? Sure, your company does, but you are responsible for hard-core growth results: marketing and new product development.

So start thinking about diversity that way. And if you do, you will elevate the value of diversity far beyond the words in the employee handbook. In fact, you are bound to conclude:

Diversity = Sustainable Competitive Advantage

Don't take my word for it. Some of the best, and most innovative, companies—Booz Allen, Deutsche Bank, DuPont, Pfizer and Raytheon—believe diversity to be one of the invaluable ingredients that leads to sustainable competitive advantage.

The argument breaks into three parts:

1. Understanding. If your workforce mirrors the diverse demographics and cultural aspects of your customers, you are bound to have a better understanding of your audience. (Providing you encourage all those unique voices to contribute. If all you are doing is counting heads—"let's see, we employ 53 percent women, 11 percent blacks, 16 percent Hispanics … yep, we're covered; now let's have the same old people at the top make all the decisions as they always have in the same old ways"—you haven't gained a thing.)

2. Credibility. If your workforce looks like the people you are trying to reach, you increase the odds of closing the sale. Let's use a simple example to make the point. From whom would 22-year-old guys want to buy their $90 athletic shoes? A 63-year-old grandmother or another 22-year-old guy?

3. Connectedness. And if your workforce is the same as the people you are trying to reach, you are bound to be closer to them at all times, which gives you a leg up on the competition.

The takeaway is clear: diversity makes a company more capable—because you are adding more skills—and smarter—because you are drawing on more and different brains. It provides a different lens that allows us to see the world in a different way. The more (different) inputs we have to work with, the better chance we have to make connections.

Talent, brains, curiosity and creativity are all race/gender/ethnicity agnostic, and an indispensable part of your innovation success. We recommend you don't innovate without as many different viewpoints as possible. That—and not some government mandate—is why diversity is important.

OUTSIDE IN-NOVATION

At the root of Zen philosophy is the ability to objectify your situation—to be able to step outside of it so you can see it for what it really is. So now that you see yourself in the jar, what do you do about it?

Here are three simple tips:

1. Get experts from beyond your industry to help you stay honest and see what is happening outside the jar. Whatever your challenge, there is an expert in a parallel industry willing to help you overcome it. Let me give you an example of what I mean by a parallel industry.

Let's say you sell something as seemingly pedestrian as furniture polish. It cleans, protects and restores. Now, what other things do that? Well, oral care and skin care products are the first two that come to mind.

Armed with this realization, how do you gain another perspective? You could forge all kinds of formal relationships with other companies, but you don't have to do that. You can simply call an expert at an oral care or cosmetic company and ask to pick his or her brain.

2. Act like an anthropologist. As I wrote earlier, an essential ingredient to innovation (and a key ability of the Idea Monkey) is the ability to objectify any situation, to be able to step back from where you are in order to gain context. Using experts from beyond your industry is a huge help in doing that.

So is going outside the office and acting like an anthropologist. Bring along a couple of members of your team, an outside expert or two, and spend time with your customer. Compare notes; you will be shocked at how differently you all see the situation.

3. Be very careful about the language you use. In this case, "voice of the customer" should be taken literally. Customers recognize, respond to and build from their own words more than yours. So use their language when exploring insights, writing concepts and introducing new products. I mentioned the insurance industry as an example earlier. But think about it. When was the last time you heard someone in your family use the word "wellness"? Yet healthcare companies can't say it enough. They are in the jar too.

Intelligence is learning from your mistakes.

Wisdom is learning from the mistakes of others. When it comes to innovation, wisdom is faster and less painful.
— GMM

Sure, you have smart people. But so does the company down the street. Simply being smart doesn't give you an edge. It's just the price of entry in Innovationland.

The best, most innovative companies are discovering that their capacity to create industry-changing products and services is directly tied to their ability to forge connections efficiently between big brains not only throughout their organization, as we just talked about, but also around the world.

It turns out the old networking cliché is also true when it comes to innovation: it's not what you know, but who you know.

The two benefits are obvious: you access additional expertise and you generate momentum. (There is nothing like introducing your smart people to someone else's to spark all kinds of ideas.)

But there are other benefits that get overlooked. For one thing, you gain objectivity. Someone from the outside can say the atomic-powered buggy whip that your R&D people are in love with is simply not going to work. In addition, those outsiders can give you a different perspective you may desperately need.

Here's an example. For years, oral care companies have relied on dentists to help fill their innovation pipelines. These companies cut their teeth (sorry!) in the professional channels, so naturally they believe dentists know more about oral care than anyone. After all, dentists spend their days talking to people about teeth, looking at teeth, thinking about teeth. So, if "four out of five" dentists think a new product idea is good, it must be, right?

Not necessarily. The world has changed. When you ask people about their mouths today, it turns out they don't talk much about cavities. They talk about sparkly teeth and fresh breath. The mouth is no longer just about dental health, it's about image. Stopping cavities is a must-have, not a game changer.

If you are looking to create innovation in oral care, you need to see it through the lens of aestheticians, stylists and fashion experts. To gain insights into what toothbrushes and toothpaste should deliver today, you need to forge relationships with people in all those fields.

How? You simply pick up the phone and call a stylist or fashion expert and ask to pick his brain.

Everyone loves to be seen as an expert. Think about it. Isn't it flattering when someone asks you: "Can you help me?" Ask those people: "What opportunities do you see? What are the emerging trends?" You aren't a competitor, so odds are they will help, especially when you offer to share what you have learned with them. You want to create these kinds of partnerships to spur new thinking and draw connections to things you might not think are related.

Examples of how connections can create innovation are all around us. The drive-in movie inspired the drive-in bank; the ballpoint pen led to roll-on deodorant; and the environment-inspired Velcro—Mother Nature calls it the cocklebur.

To paraphrase innovation guru Roger von Oech, "connection is the father of conception." Start connecting.

"Did you get approval from legal? And operations? And Wally? And Asia? ... "

LIST THREE BENEFITS YOUR PRODUCT OR SERVICE
DELIVERS (e.g., it enhances, it protects and it conditions).

> _____

> _____

> _____

NOW, LIST THREE OTHER INDUSTRIES, PRODUCTS OR
SERVICES THAT COULD MAKE THESE SAME CLAIMS.

> _____

> _____

> _____

THINK: WHAT CAN YOU LEARN FROM THEM?

(RING)LEADER To-Dos

Look in the mirror and remind yourself that **you are inside the jar.**

Question everything like a five-year-old.

When you notice yourself thinking that you know all there is to know, **have the Monkey work with you** to turn every assumption on its head.

Diversify your inputs by engaging diverse individuals and/or rotating–creating new perspectives by swapping roles or switching departments.

Network for knowledge outside of your company with thought leaders from parallel industries.

(Doodle something here that would
make your 4th grade teacher wince.)

Chapter 5
Laugh a Little, Innovate a Lot

Fear is the mortal enemy of creativity, innovation and happiness.
—Alex Bogusky, advertising "it" boy

How much fun are you having at work these days?

Let's face it. Having fun isn't as easy as it used to be, even for the most courageous, creative and curious. Today, just reading the headlines can turn an energetic optimist into a fearful pessimist.

Here is something that I discovered many years ago. **It is impossible to innovate effectively if you are afraid.** Impossible. Nothing kills great ideas like fear.

So if you are an innovation leader—(Ring)leader or Idea Monkey—in a company that has become fearful, your people are on the road to failure unless you can change your culture.

The good news is that fun is the antidote to fear. Cue the circus music; it's time to infuse some fun into the workplace.

The place to start? With you.

Leaders know how to laugh at themselves. Show us a person who can stand up in front of his team and say, "Call me stupid, but I have no idea how to do this," and we will show you a person with great leadership potential. Humble leaders create cultures that don't take themselves too seriously, cultures willing to take risks, cultures capable of creating and supporting a greater number of ideas.

GENERAL SILLINESS

We don't just talk about silliness. We live it. We have the ping pong table; we have a stage with a complete set of rock band equipment ready to go.  In fact, one of the highest compliments we ever received was being kindly called "daddy day care" by one of our team member's kids.

As you can imagine, Maddock Douglas has a history of memorable events designed to loosen people up, not take ourselves so seriously, and, uh, have fun at work. For the sake of inspiration as well as the betterment of idea circles everywhere, I'll share a few of my favorites:

The Unmotivational Speaker

We assembled our entire company for a "full-day" meeting to hear from a "World Famous Motivational Speaker." The speaker was actually John Wartinbee, the senior vice president of a local bank. John is a naturally funny guy who was pushing 70. My only instructions to John: "Be the most ridiculously bad motivational speaker you can be. Leave it all in the room." So for over an hour, our folks looked nervously at the partners in the company as John:

- called us the wrong names; Wes was "Russ," Mike was "Mack" …
- looked at the watch on his left hand and said he was running incredibly late so he had to pick things up, then, moments later, looked at the watch on his right hand that would cause him to say he was way ahead of schedule.
- quoted convicted felons from books telling us to "think about that, and try to live your life that way."

- constantly jingled the keys, candy, coins and toys in each of his pockets. Occasionally he'd take an item out, give a curious "Hmpphh?" and then keep talking.
- put hard candy in his mouth and slur his speech.
- passed out plastic rulers, scissors, tape, etc., that had "Property of Sacred Heart Catholic School" written on each item ... then forget why he passed out the items.

John basically made absolutely no sense—with heartfelt conviction—for the better part of an hour. He laughed, he cried and he looked confused. And so did every person at Maddock Douglas. All the while, Wes Douglas and I looked nervously at each other, playing along.

After we had suffered enough, John led us down to the parking lot for a "team-building" exercise. There, the ruse ended and we asked everyone to jump into buses waiting to take us all to an amusement park for the day. Thank you, John. You were spectacular!

The Silly Olympics

June is time for the annual company picnic. As you might imagine, we try to make every picnic a bit different. My favorite one included the Silly Olympics. Teams competed for gold in events they designed. Some of my favorites:

- **Who Cut the Cheese?** A relay race in which teams raced to a chair, sat on a whoopie cushion, ate a piece of cheese, then ran back, spraying air freshener.
- **Blindfolded Oven Mitt Card Grab.** 60 seconds to grab as many playing cards as you can wearing oven mitts.
- **Olive Oil Egg Toss.** Man those things are slippery!

The Sweet Feet (aka: Testicle Spectacle)

What happens when a young man says, "I am the fastest guy in the office," in the presence of four other guys? Two pulled hamstrings, a seriously skinned knee, a YouTube video, a "face plant,"

and weeks of unrelenting hazing. In case you are wondering, the braggart was proven very wrong.

Design Your Own Scooter

One of our clients wound up with a whole mess of Razor Scooters left over from a promotion. They asked if we'd like some for our kids. We had another idea. We organized the company into teams of five and had a scooter decorating contest. Points were given for music, costume and general scooter silliness. Entries included:

- The Flintstone scooter—complete with a coconut candle headlight and a leopard skin costume.
- The California low-rider scooter—decorated with bling, red shag carpet and a rider covered in do-rags.
- And the not-to-be-forgotten "Daddy got me a pony" scooter—my personal favorite.

You can still ride these scooters around our office. A nice memory of a great party and childlike creativity.

THE DAILY HUDDLE

Why not start every day with a fun meeting? The daily huddle is a simple practice that jump-starts the day and sets the stage for big ideas. Verne Harnish, "growth guy" and chief executive officer of Gazelles, which is an outsourced corporate university for midsize firms, taught us about the daily huddle. He developed the practice after studying and writing about John D. Rockefeller in his book *The Rockefeller Habits*. Here is our variation on Verne's idea. Our company meets every day at 9 a.m. for no more than nine minutes. The agenda for our 9@9 meeting is simple. We share good news, "stucks" and keymetrics. We use video to connect offices so everyone can attend the meeting. We encourage everyone to take a turn at running the huddle. Most importantly, we try to make them casual, transparent and fun.

In the last year, our daily huddles have included baby pools— where everyone guesses when someone's baby will be born, whether it will be a boy or girl, and what it will weigh—costume contests, music trivia, engagement announcements, love poems, and ballads to welcome new employees. Yes, there is a lot of silliness and, not surprisingly, there is a lot of laughter. Much of the laughter has led to jokes, observations and comments that have, in turn, led to ideas that have directly impacted our clients, company and community.

Says Harnish, "Of all the practices we teach, the daily huddle is probably the simplest and most powerful way to infuse fun, accountability and momentum. When companies embrace the huddle, we always see a positive impact to their bottom line and culture."

He's right. In fact, our clients actually like to come to these huddles. That should tell you something about the experience.

The "Out the Scott" Birthday

Joe Kim is a shareholder in the firm who, in a former life, was a diversity coach. Joe is 100 percent Asian. Korean to be exact. He looks the part and proudly lets everyone in on his heritage.

O'Kim Family Crest

On the morning of Joe's birthday, I walked into his office, gave him a classic Scottish costume, and asked him to play along and put it on. At our 9@9 meeting, I made the startling announcement that Joe's wife had told me that Joe was not Korean. He was actually Scottish. We then unveiled his family crest—filled with as many Asian cliches as possible—and then ushered in a bagpipe player to regale us with stories about the famous "Kim" family and play the Kim family song.

(Note: this would have been absolutely offensive in the wrong environment with the wrong person. Credit goes to Joe and our culture that doesn't take itself too seriously.)

(Note 2: being overly PC can also kill ideas ... but I digress.)

LOOSENING UP THE SUITS

We first started noticing the liberating possibilities of linking fun and work in the early '90s in a meeting with an extremely conservative, extremely large utility company. You have probably been in a similar room—think suits; think fear; think awkward silence.

During this "mandatory" brainstorm session, someone offered up an idea as a joke. "I know," he said, tongue firmly in cheek. "We can send customers a bill that actually explains all of the charges in plain English." He meant it as a joke, of course. And one joke led to another. Then something amazing happened: at one point the most senior person in the room commented, "You know, that's really not that bad of an idea. We could actually do that." Eventually the idea that started as a joke wound up being seen by 40 million consumers as a new kind of phone bill—one that was simple to understand. Not only did consumers embrace the joke, so did AT&T and SBC, who have adopted the same idea. How great is that?

When looking for a big idea, you don't necessarily want to hear "Eureka!" but laughter.

THE EQUATION

There are two lessons here. First, it is not difficult to stage events that create this type of result, and leaders should create them. More importantly, we must learn to pay attention to laughter. Where there is laughter, there is an idea that holds people's interest. The pleasant by-product of all this: work becomes more enjoyable, and that, too, increases the chance that you will be able to innovate successfully. If you are having fun, you are more creative.

Here is an equation for you to consider the next time you are wondering why nobody is coming up with big ideas:

$$I = F + H$$

Ideas equal fun plus humility on the part of leadership to support the idea. As a leader, you are in charge of the "F" and the "H." If you take care of those, your team will take care of the rest.

Sinnovation

Invariably, when we want to deliver a warning or even cautionary advice, we always cast it in the negative. "Don't do this."

It is a perfectly valid approach, one that is as old as the Bible. After all, eight of the Ten Commandments are presented in some version of "thou shall not."

But you can get the same thoughts across using humor. So why not consider the Seven Deadly Sins of the Innovator? (We've seen all of these cause failures of biblical proportions.)

If she were a creativity consultant, I am certain Sister Nancy would tell you not to commit these sins.

Lust: which in our world means innovating in a space you have no business being in. Innovating outside your operational expertise or brand footprint creates incredible inertia internally—"should I be working on the things I should be working on, or the harebrained scheme that someone else higher up on the org chart has conjured up?"—and unhealthy confusion externally. "Wait," the customer says. "My long-time supplier of plastic molding ejection equipment is now making iPhone accessories? What gives?" Most innovation success involves complementary products, services and business models because they are readily accepted by your team and make sense to your customers. "Stick to your knitting" is excellent advice until a solid business case proves otherwise. Mother Teresa said, "Grow where you are planted." She was really smart.

 **Gluttony:** trying to do too many initiatives with too little resources. Innovation takes emotional and financial capital and focus. Venture capitalists can afford to back 10 companies, hoping that payoff from one or two will cover the expense of having the other eight or nine investments fail, but odds are you can't. Instead of making a number of small bets, focus your team and resources on one or two initiatives that have the greatest probability of hitting it big.

Greed: taking short-term profits at the expense of long-term growth. The stock market demands a high rate of return that naturally results in safe bets like line extensions. Line extensions are fine, but they leave you at risk of being blown out of the water by an industry-changing idea. The solution? Create two teams. Put an internal one in

Short term profits at the expense of long term growth

charge of evolution and the other, partnered with outside experts, in charge of revolution. You'll get both short- and long-term growth.

Sloth: which we define as not doing the hard work; not following the proven process; taking shortcuts. Too many otherwise brilliant leaders have made the mistake of thinking that speed and shortcuts are the only way to innovation success. While we agree that being overly cautious—"let's test the idea for the 83rd time"—is also potentially fatal, there is a happy medium. Think big, quantify, qualify, refine and launch. This should take no more than 12 months. If you can do it in eight, great! If you can do it in three, then you have left something out—or you have a very, very tired staff on your hands. Remember: just because it takes one woman nine months to have a baby doesn't mean that nine women can produce one in 30 days.

"One more test and I think we have our winner!"

Wrath: being so focused on your competition that you miss the same opportunities that they are missing. If you concentrate on what they are doing, you are both going to get your butt kicked from someone outside your industry who is rightly focused on the consumer (and not either one of you).

Envy: in the context of innovation, it means launching a "me-too" product instead of finding a space you could own. An example of envy is when your sales team comes to you and demands that you launch a product to compete with the "hot" new offering they just saw from the competitor. Don't take the bait. Chances are that product is going to fail. Instead, use your sales team to find out what other needs your customer or consumer has and attack them with your own novel product, service or business model.

This other one is nothing more than a "me-too" product.

Pride: you won't give up on your favorite idea—even when the numbers prove you are wrong. **Hey boss, this one is for you.** Nobody wants to tell you that you are wrong, which means that, especially when it comes to your ideas, *you must* look at the data. Unless it is overwhelmingly in favor of your idea, drop it and work on the one that the team secretly knows is better. You'll make more money and keep the respect of your team.

Religion tells us the seven deadly sins are fatal to spiritual progress. We will let you debate that thought with the theologian of your choice. We do know, however, that they are definitely fatal if you want to innovate successfully.

Take extreme care to guard against them.

Honesty Check: I'm going to work on ...	
☐ **Lust**	Working on ideas that don't play to our strengths
☐ **Gluttony**	Doing too much at once
☐ **Greed**	Focusing only on short-term profits
☐ **Sloth**	Taking too many shortcuts
☐ **Wealth**	Letting competition fog my perspective
☐ **My Wardrobe**	Let's face it ... it's time

(RING)LEADER To-Dos

Don't be a stick in the mud. No one feels comfortable laughing if the boss is a pig.

Why do you want to laugh a little at work? That's simple.

Fun is the antidote to fear.

Whenever possible, don't say "thou shall not" or even "don't." You can get the same message across by using positive (and even fun) language.

(Please take notes here to make authors believe
they are actually delivering some value.)

(Thank you.)

Chapter 6

I Fail, Therefore I Am
(an innovator)

Columbus insisted the world was round and then promptly missed America on his first attempt. The Wright Brothers claimed flying was possible and nearly killed themselves trying to prove it. And, of course, Albert Einstein, whose very name we use as a shorthand for "genius," was a lousy student.

Our point: failure isn't fatal; in fact, it is actually *required* for innovation success.

If you study the pattern of companies that have a history of introducing new products successfully, you will see they follow a pattern that looks like this: try, fail, learn; try, fail, learn; try, succeed, repeat. All that failure—all those introductions of versions of a product or service that just don't work—is a critical cultural attribute for successful, fast-growth companies.

"Failure is part of my success." This is an idea you need to accept if you are going to do your best work, and it is an idea you definitely have to get across to your team in order to free it from the innovation-limiting shackles of perfection. You need to make failure a positive part of everyone's personal brands.

INNOVATION IS ITERATIVE

Great innovation, like great people, typically is not born, it is raised. The phrase, "Be patient, God isn't finished with me yet" is a healthy mantra for most of us—and most innovation projects. One reason that's true is that in order to make a product or service everything it can be, it needs to be repeatedly soft-launched. This means literally sending the idea—be it a product or a service—into a limited part of the marketplace with the full understanding that it will be modified (perhaps extensively) based on how consumers react.

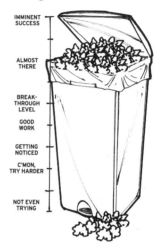

A Sign of Success

IMMINENT SUCCESS

ALMOST THERE

BREAK-THROUGH LEVEL

GOOD WORK

GETTING NOTICED

C'MON, TRY HARDER

NOT EVEN TRYING

"'Success' usually marks the end of an endeavor, whereas failure is the signal for another advancement."

"'Courage' is going from failure to failure without losing enthusiasm."
—Winston Churchill

For successful launches to happen, a team must be okay with the premise that they are starting with what some may consider a half-baked idea; one that very well may fail as constituted. You need to make this okay. You need to tell your team that the real failure is fear of launching an idea until it is perfect.

Should the "No Child Left Behind" Act really be called "No Child Gets Ahead"?

I would argue that when nobody is allowed to fail (spectacularly), we are failing our kids.

To buttress your case, make the following points:

1. We're only right when the market tells us so. Right now, we presume to be right and our thinking is based on as-good-as-we-can-get research, history and gut feel. The market will help us see and hear what we can do to be more right (and also help us eliminate all the things our customers—and potential customers—don't like or don't want).

2. We can make any changes quickly. We can simulate years of research data in the span of months once we are out in the marketplace. It is the fastest way to learn.

3. It has never been cheaper to test ideas. The Internet allows for instant feedback; empty strip malls allow for in-and-out shopping experiences with risk-free, short-term leases; storefronts are often now virtual, which means you can test the product and marketing real time; technology has made prototyping doable in days instead of months; online panels give you an instant read on the market.

4. It will be fun. We're doing this to learn and improve, not to beat up an idea. (So there is no reason for anyone to get defensive.)

5. We will be making our "mistake" on a small scale, i.e., we are not launching the Iridium Phone or Segway only to find no one understands it or only 1,000 people want it. If we find out our idea is completely off base, we'll save the company millions of dollars and perhaps our jobs.

> TODAY,
> "WORD-OF-MOUTH"
> IS ACTUALLY
> TRACKABLE AND
> MEASURABLE

One more point: be careful with the language you use when describing your testing process. We often find that words like "prototype" and "beta" come with too much baggage to overcome. When they hear those terms, many people think it means certain elements of the product (or service) you are about to test are locked in place. That's not the message you want to send. Just about everything should be up for grabs. For our people, "soft launch" means we expect lots of things about the idea to change. But consider creating your own language that stresses the results you are trying to achieve, e.g., "iteration phase 3" or "project optimize." If your team still resists the idea of iterative soft launches, just remind them that if this approach was good enough for Columbus and the Wright brothers, it is probably good enough for them.

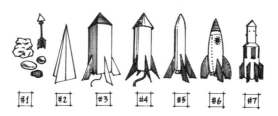

LEARN FROM HISTORY

"Those who cannot remember the past are condemned to repeat it," wrote philosopher George Santayana.

Most of us know that, and that's why we study the magazine stories, business review articles and books written about successful companies. We want to know what worked.

But when a once-innovative company gets into trouble, it's easy to start thinking that its business model was fatally flawed and there's nothing to be learned from the company's history. And that, as Santayana pointed out, is a huge mistake.

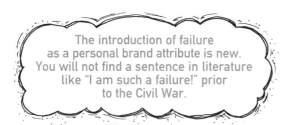

The introduction of failure as a personal brand attribute is new. You will not find a sentence in literature like "I am such a failure!" prior to the Civil War.

An upstart home builder, who happens to be a former client of ours, is not making that mistake. He is learning from the once-great Ford Motor Company. With all the troubles Ford is going through, it is easy to forget just how innovative Henry Ford was.

To understand just how clever he was, let's go back to the late 1800s. You want one of those newfangled horseless carriages that everyone is talking about. So you meet with a person who draws one up for you. You talk about the size, what it will look like, what kinds of bells and whistles yours will include, and how it will be nicer than the guy's across the street. You make a deposit. Months pass. Your designer comes back with drawings. You make changes. When you finally agree on the design, a team of craftsmen get to work building you a car. Flash forward to 1908. Henry Ford, with a magnificent stroke of process innovation, puts most carmakers out of business almost overnight with the introduction of the Model T, which was produced on an assembly line, not by hand.

Now let's consider the housing industry. It has been 100 years since Ford changed things. You want one of those "green" homes that everyone is talking about. So you meet with a person who draws one up for you. You talk about the size, what it will look like, what kinds of bells and whistles yours will include, and how it will be nicer than the guy's across the street. You make a deposit. Months pass. Your designer comes back to you with drawings. You make changes. When you finally agree on the design, a team of craftsmen get to work building you a new home. Sound familiar?

Where's Henry Ford when you need him?

Enter Rick Lavers. We met Rick Lavers when he was the CEO of All American Homes, a company that is doing to homes what Ford Motor did to cars. I predict that companies like All American Homes will put traditional home builders out of business in the same way Ford was responsible for winnowing the car industry a century ago. Why? They assemble houses just like Ford built cars: on an indoor assembly line that frees construction from the vagaries of the weather and allows them to build 24 hours a day.

Why am I excited about this innovation? Because by centralizing manufacturing, innovation can go into warp speed. Think about where the car industry would be today if all the builders were craftsmen spread out across the country. Building cars in central locations makes possible experimentation, improvements and learning every day.

So the takeaway seems clear: if you don't learn from history, you just may become extinct—an irony that was recently almost wasted on the competitors of Ford Motor.

Introducing new products and services successfully requires: a) sufficient expertise and resources, b) a defined process and c) leadership resolve.

But talking about expertise, process and resolve is boring to everyone except engineers (and people who introduce new products successfully). So, with apologies to David Letterman, here's my list of the top 10 reasons why your next new launch will fail.

10. Science Run Amok. Companies use their research and development capabilities to come up with unique products, instead of making customer needs their starting point. They begin with what they are good at, as opposed to what customers want. I will readily admit that there are many examples of revolutionary innovation that started as a novel technology, but this isn't repeatable. For you to create an innovation machine, you must start with the notion that new products aren't bloodhounds that go find markets. They must address an unmet need.

The Orange Shag Rule

After graduating college, I rented a home that would eventually accommodate three friends and two dogs. Three years later, I married my bride and we decided to rehab the place. The first thing she wanted to change was the pole in our living room that she said was covered with orange shag carpeting. "What pole?" I asked. I insisted that it didn't exist. After four years, I could no longer see it.

Research proves that people don't see things unless they are looking for them. As a leader, you have the opportunity to help your team find the orange shag—to fix things they no longer see as broken.

9. The Lemming Effect. "The competition has just introduced an X, so we need to have an X, too." If all you are offering is a me-too product, you can only gain market share by cutting price, and who wants to go that route? Find an unmet need and go after it.

8. "Team ACME." See if this sounds familiar. Someone comes up with an idea and it gets implemented by an ad hoc team with money found in a slush fund. It's a daring approach. It's innovative. And it almost never works because it isn't sufficiently thought out. If you have ever watched a Wile E. Coyote  cartoon, you understand the problem. The Coyote's ad hoc solutions to the problem of catching the Road Runner seem on the surface to make sense, but they always contain a fatal flaw that causes them to blow up in the end. If you substitute your company for Wile E. and "a nagging consumer challenge" for the Road Runner, you'll see why there are better ways to go. Meep Meep.

7. It's Scary Out There. There are thousands of reasons not to be bold. The economy is weak; the market is unsettled. Somebody needs a hug. Fine, go get yourself one. Then buck up and get aggressive.

Many people believe America is the most inventive country. Ironically, it turns out that we may have invented fear of failure. According to Scott A. Sandage, a professor of history at Carnegie Mellon University, only recently have we used failure as something that defines one's identity. Could this be why we have so much trouble embracing failure?

Scott argues that people being branded by their failure is tied directly to entrepreneurial capitalism in 19th century America. Prior to 1820, there were no police reports, credit reports or report cards to follow you around. For the first time in history, the story of your life—and your associated failures—could actually hurt you.

Whether you believe that success and failure as personal as brand attributes is a recent development or not, this much is true: in America, everything we do is now put in the success or failure box. After twenty years of working with the biggest companies and best thinkers, I can assure you that the fear of failure is killing innovation.

6. The Market Is Too Small. For a new product to be successful, you need sufficient sales. It sounds ridiculously obvious, doesn't it? But you would be amazed at the number of companies that design a product for too small a market. Say your new product is targeted at households with at least $55,000 in annual income. Well, that's only 50 percent of the 105 million U.S. households. But it's  really just for the 18-65 age groups—that eliminates another third. And this mythical product will only appeal to those with an active lifestyle: one-third of the remaining 35 million homes—some 12 million. Say you get 33 percent to try it, and of those four million households, only 50 percent say they would buy it again. Your potential market is about two million households, and sales at that level won't cover the developmental costs, advertising, etc. Instead of acknowledging this, we redefine the market as "for everyone 18 and over"—and then wonder why a product designed for a narrow target didn't sell well.

Related to the size of the market is the size of your innovation budget. Revolutionary innovation creates disruption in the market *and* within your company. Changing the way your company works is expensive, and a typical innovation budget does not consider this cost. Leaders *must* consider the holistic benefits of change and budget accordingly.

5. Dartboard Product Design. There is almost never sufficient thought given to what the total product should look like. Let's say there are four key components—price, packaging, size and usability—that could affect how well it sells. And each one of them has four options. So there are 256 different ways you could manufacture that product. What's the predominant technique used to choose among them? People sit around a conference table with some pizza and soft drinks and say, about a new paper towel, for example, "Let's go with 500 sheets, super-high absorbency, middle-of-the-road packaging and priced 10 percent above the market leader." What's the probability they've chosen right? By definition, it is 1 out of 256. Maybe they have some expertise. That boosts the odds to 1:128. Better, but still not great.

4. Death By Consensus. If everyone has to agree on the key characteristics of a new product, you are going to end up introducing really bland products. The higher the number of people who have to agree, the worse this gets. Create a small task force of new product experts and empower them. Let them live (or die) by how often they are right. You will get more compelling ideas to market faster.

3. No One Told The Higher Ups. You have a great idea. But because your process did not identify key stakeholders and influencers, it is your idea, not everyone's. Want to see your boss kill an awesome idea? Fail to include him early and often.

2. Leadership Churn. You have a great idea, but you turn it over to others who don't care as much as you do. As we have said throughout, the people who come up with the idea need to see it through to the marketplace. Ideas need parents.

1. Ready, Fire, Aim. Speed to market is a killer concept in the negative sense. It kills new products. You don't want to make your mistakes in public. To launch a product before it is ready with a $40 million campaign is just idiotic. The problem is, it isn't seen as idiotic. It's seen as one of the costs of doing business. That's sad. Repeatedly test your product in limited markets and refine after each test.

BELIEVE IN INNOVATION TO WIN

There is no doubt most companies today are big believers in the idea of innovation. Its importance is heralded in corporate visions and mission statements. The CEO speaks its glory in almost every speech, and its importance is celebrated on internal posters as well as in the company's marketing materials.

So how come we're not being overwhelmed by innovative new products and services?

Unfortunately, that's simple to answer.

Saying you believe in something is one thing. Living what you believe is another. Most companies don't believe in innovation enough to do much more than pretend.

You can see the proof of that in three approaches companies typically take to try to show the world they're innovative:

1. The big sweeping announcement. "Five years from now, we will get 50 percent (or some other big number) of our revenues from products that don't exist today," the chairman announces with great fanfare. Everyone applauds, and then  absolutely nothing changes about the way the company does business.

2. Let's make a list. The company hires an ideation company to help it brainstorm all the things it might want to add innovation to, and then nothing happens primarily because of people who say things like "I would have loved to do something with that list, but I had to keep doing my day job."

3. The innovation drive-by. The organization hires a company like ours to help it create a new product quickly. But like anything new within the company, it ends up being mired in internal politics, bureaucracy ("Whose budget do we charge for this?") and turf wars.

4. The kinda-rogue department. Company leadership empowers a single department to innovate on an island. The challenge is that typically they will only create concepts that they have the power to enact. For example, in insurance, innovation often needs buy-in from claims, underwriting, etc. These are typically different departments. If they were not part of the original idea, their only remaining power may be to say "no."

Why don't companies make innovation an essential part of the way they do business? Because it's hard. Because it requires an unwavering, wholehearted leap of faith—backed by a major investment, not only of money, but of people, processes and infrastructure. It requires audacious goals, evangelism, consistency, education, training, diversity, expert tools, expert processes and an environment conducive to creating sustainable innovation results that are aligned with financial outcomes.

The world's most innovative companies—think Google, GE, Nike and Procter & Gamble—demonstrate that innovation is an essential part of their organization by giving it the same level of status, clout, equality and attention as they do their fundamental core competencies (e.g., operations, customer service, quality). They not only embrace failure, they have made it core to their process. They have created a culture where the Idea Monkeys are swinging past each failure toward success and (Ring) leaders are focusing them on which failures are the most informative and most valuable. Show me a culture that embraces and learns from failure and I'll show you an innovative company.

TIP: Document your failures as well as your successes.

Failing forward–that is, learning from your mistakes – is not a bad thing. You should be able to take your partners through the systematic and intentional pattern of how you get to success. Show how you test, improve and launch your products, services and business models. This is incredibly powerful and reassuring to investors, employees and the marketplace in general.

THE TOP FIVE REASONS IDEAS GET STUCK
IN MY COMPANY/LIFE:

> _____

> _____

> _____

> _____

> _____

(RING)LEADER To-Dos

Make failure a positive part of your culture to overcome the inherent fear of failure—celebrate failing forward. Monkeys will feel liberated if you do.

Document your failures and your successes.

Create a list of failures that you learned from the most.

Maximize what you learn by sharing it across the organization.

At Maddock Douglas, we strongly support protecting white space. Thank you for understanding.

Chapter 7

How to Produce
Big Ideas on Demand

Freeing your mind to think in an innovative way can
be as easy as jumping in the shower and tuning out.

What if I told you that you could come up with a great idea
anytime you wanted?

I'll go further. I can show you how to not only summon new and
innovative concepts on command, but also how to teach your people
the same skill.

This may sound like an infomer-
cial ("Order our revolutionary system within the next 20 minutes, and
we'll throw in this set of steak knives
absolutely free!"), but it's true.

Here's why. You undoubtedly
have too much on your mind. It's
like driving during rush hour; you
are too busy dealing with traffic to
notice the scenery and enjoy the ride.

The following practices eliminate mental traffic and help you liberate the great ideas inside you desperately trying to get out. The following five techniques outlined have two things in common: they free
your brain to let your best ideas flow, and they are techniques we've
seen our most creative resources use again and again successfully.

1. Shower your way to creativity. Yep, it's absolutely true. There is a scientific theory that says, water hitting your head helps trigger the synapses and that's why people get great ideas in the shower. But I think it's simpler than that. The ideas occur because you are not making an effort to think. You aren't worried about anything. You are not stressed. Hence some of your best thinking occurs.

CREATIVITY SHOWER

2. Sleep on it. Remember how your mom used to say, "Why don't you sleep on it, honey?" when you were wrestling with a big issue? Well, when it comes to big ideas and problem solving, mother really does know best.

The next time you want to solve a major challenge or be unusually brilliant, think about it in bed. Don't push yourself to figure out the answer before you fall asleep. Instead, just go through the issues at hand and tell yourself that you will have the answer in the morning. In my experience, this technique amplifies the power of the shower, because there are even fewer distractions to occupy your mind when you are asleep.

Build on this idea: You can employ an alternate version of this while awake. The next time you can't think of a name, date or important fact, just tell yourself aloud, "I will not think about this for awhile,

and the answer will come to me." This technique clears the traffic in your mind and lets your subconscious go to work. Your answer will often pop into your head the moment you stop "thinking about it."

> Thomas Edison, Leonardo de Vinci and Albert Einstein all reportedly took short naps during the day to rest their conscious mind and let the subconscious go to work.

3. Open streams of consciousness. Purging is a great way to make new connections and create bigger ideas.

Have a tough challenge to solve? Get a giant piece of paper (write small if you can't find one). In each quarter of the paper, write a key word related to the challenge. For example, if you want to plan a cool family vacation, you might write the words "destinations," "transportation," "kids" and "fun."

Then, in no particular order, begin to brainstorm any word that comes to mind when you think of each of the key words. For example, for "transportation": plane, train, automobile, John Candy, pillows, sleep, sleeping bag, tent, tree house, memories, dreams, daydreams, smells, popcorn, movies, adventure, pirates, islands, Swiss Family Robinson. Eventually, you will begin to make connections, and ideas that unify the key aspects of your goal will pop off the page.

(Imagine how much fun you'll have explaining to your family how you came up with the idea of renting a tree house for your vacation in Costa Rica. They didn't see that one coming.)

Remember: Strive for as many words as you can, and don't judge the words. Judging is looking at the traffic when you are driving—it keeps you from coming up with ideas. Eliminate the traffic.

You can employ this simple technique yourself or do it in groups.

Build on this idea: You can also do this at work.

4. Schedule your daydreaming. We all have a time of day when our brains work the best. For many, it is first thing in the morning, before rush hour. Unfortunately, the CrackBerry addiction has many of us checking our e-mail just when our brains are the most capable of creating.

Tip: Professional trainers track the exercise regiments of athletes, charting at what time of day they are at their strongest and/or have the most energy. One reason they do this is to identify each athlete's natural cycle so they can push them harder at just the right time.

The creative brain has natural cycles too. Start by tracking when you think the best. What time of day is it? What time of the month? What activities were you doing when you had the big idea? Learn to save your toughest challenges for the times when your brain is at peak performance.

"All the really good ideas I ever had came to me while I was milking a cow."
—Grant Wood

The moment you check your e-mail, voice mail or to-do list, you have hijacked your imagination. You have created a mental traffic jam. Do yourself a favor and schedule daydreaming. Unplug during the time that you know you do your best thinking and find a place that makes you feel energized. A lot of people love the local coffee shop. The buzz of conversation, the smells, colors and energy create a safe haven for the mind to wander. Some prefer the library or the park. Whichever it is, go there. Let your mind take off.

5. Yuck it up! Laughing is another great way to liberate your brain. Often, consciously doing silly-seeming things will get the creative juices flowing. Spin a top. Get an ice cream cone.

As you test these five techniques, you'll find some work better than others. If it turns out you really do get your best ideas in the shower, be conscious of the circumstances under which they occurred. What was the water temperature like? How long had you been in there? What time was it? Replicate the experience—daily. You'll find the effort worthwhile.

"The bottom line is that gifted performers are almost always made, not born, and that the journey to superior performance is for neither the faint of heart nor the impatient," says Rand Stagen, senior partner of Stagen, a leadership consulting firm that specializes in helping mid-market companies scale. "Just as in sports, becoming an elite performer in business requires struggle, sacrifice and honest (often painful) self-assessment. Depending on the scope and difficulty of the skill to be learned, it will take months and probably years to achieve a high level of proficiency or mastery." Said differently: practice will make you a better Idea Monkey or a better (Ring)leader. Even the most creative thinkers and managers

can improve themselves through intentional practices. In fact, learning how to implement simple approaches like these are often what separates a brilliant thinker from a creative want-to-be. Really. At first, you may feel silly, but I promise these ideas will work.

THREE NUGGETS OF SMARTS:

1. Once you have an idea you like, do not ask a committee to agree that it is a good idea. If you do, everyone will chime in with their small changes. The result?

The idea dies the death of 1,000 cuts. You'll end up with a milk toast idea dumbed-down to the point where it will lack the impact that great ideas usually have.

2. Listen to seasoned experts? "Who the hell wants to hear actors talk?" So said Harry Warner, one of the founders of the Warner Brothers, in 1927 when someone suggested adding sound to films would make them more appealing. Experts in your business aren't always experts. Instead, ask a professional "outside your jar."

3. A counterintuitive rule about rules: Most believe that the fewer rules that you have, the more innovative you can be. Actually, in my experience, the more criteria you must meet, the higher the likelihood of success. This is because criteria come from leaders who have to support your (their) ideas.

Obviously, the people you would most like to produce ideas on demand are your company's great thinkers. But who are they? (You may know some of them—among your direct reports for example—but do you know everyone organization-wide?) How do you identify and enlist your company's best and brightest—the Idea Monkey—even if they are not usually part of your company's marketing efforts?

It's easier than you may think. Here are three ideas:

Encourage Fun and Games. Your first challenge is to attract the "ideators," the people who traditionally come up with the biggest ideas, regardless of the topic. Great ideators tend to be a bit competitive. Tap into that. Post challenges—through your intranet, bulletin board or e-mail system—on behalf of clients, and offer prizes for anyone who can come up with the answer within a set period of time.

Build on this idea: We often use this technique when we are trying to name a product or service. The best names come from connecting hundreds of ideas with specific insights. So this technique really drives quantity.

Competitive, inventive people will respond with hundreds of novel ideas that you can adopt. The prize can be simple: a free lunch or sports tickets. If you have cash in the budget, even better.

If you don't have a current client project in need of solving, you can make one up. For example, if vacuum cleaners did not exist, how would you clean floors? The question isn't as important as the answers. The responses you get will give you a great list of innovative thinkers.

Encourage Graffiti. Want a simple way to foster a culture of innovation and find out who has hidden strengths? Allow people to draw on the walls. One thing that works particularly well for our firm when we are looking for new insights, or ways to tweak a product or service offering, is to paper the walls of a room with flip chart sheets. We write thought-starters and headlines that relate directly to the challenge at hand. For a vacuum project, we might post headlines like "things that pick stuff up," or "the cleanest surfaces in your house."

Then we ask everyone—no matter where they are in the organization or what their title—to drop by the room a few times and have some fun. We tell them, "Build on others' ideas." Cut out pictures. Draw. Make connections. Once the walls are filled, schedule mini-meetings where you moderate a discussion among small groups of participants to take the ideas further.

Here's the best part. You won't have to sell this idea. The room becomes a magnet. You will quickly get new ideas and you'll see who has the ability to connect, build and reinvent. This costs nothing but time and often results in astoundingly fresh thinking.

Raise Your Profile. The great thing about taking either or both of these approaches is that not only does the company benefit, but it also gives those who would like to be seen as experts opportunities to raise their hands in a nonthreatening atmosphere. If you're one of those people who is looking to raise your profile, participate in these exercises every chance you get. That will get you noticed. You will be seen as an idea catalyst, someone whose ideas, enthusiasm and energy causes others to be more energetic and engaged. People who help organizations identify and engage great thinkers are prized. And so are the great thinkers.

HARNESSING THE POWER OF THE SALES FORCE

Home runs—the big industry-changing innovations—are wonderful. But in the battle for new products and services, you need singles as well. Your sales force can be a great source of coming up with them. They love incremental improvements:

- ShinyGlow cleaner with new packaging graphics.
- ShinyGlow cleaner with a new, resealable top.
- ShinyGlow cleaner in an applicator pen.
- ShinyGlow cleaner "now with static guard."
- ShinyGlow cleaner in an easy-to-pour package.
- ShinyGlow cleaner with built-in sunshine softener.

These types of ideas are usually easy to come up with and to execute, and are often created in response to a competitor's product. If the sales group likes these incremental ideas, they tend to be successful because the salespeople work harder to make them a reality.

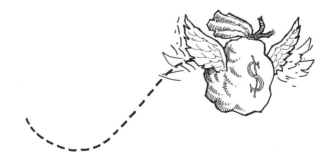

101 OTHER WAYS TO PRODUCE IDEAS ON DEMAND

1. Take a warm bath. 2. Go for a drive with the windows open. 3. Order Chinese food and eat it with chopsticks. 4. Call a random phone number—ask a stranger. 5. Ask a child. 6. Create an idea that would get you fired. 7. Paint your bedroom. 8. Consult tarot cards. 9. Gargle. 10. Play foosball. 11. Sing a show tune in a crowded elevator. 12. How would your favorite uncle solve the problem? 13. Doodle. 14. Do a crossword puzzle. 15. Pray for a little help. 16. Ask the most creative person you know. 17. Ask the least creative person you know. 18. Run. 19. Ask your local postal worker. 20. Ice skate. 21. Take a shower with your clothes on. 22. Ask yourself, "What rhymes with orange?" 23. Talk to your favorite cheerleader about the idea. 24. Breathe slowly. 25. Flip a coin. 26. Mow the lawn. 27. What is the simplest solution? 28. Do 20 quick push-ups. 29. Go shopping! 30. Write the alphabet backwards. 31. Build a fort in your office. 32. How would an ant solve the problem? 33. Create a silly solution that rhymes. 34. Make paper airplanes. 35. Use three wishes to solve your challenge. 36. Browse through a bookstore. 37. Take a survey. 38. Make a sculpture with mashed potatoes. 39. Fish. 40. Go to Vegas, play a lot of craps. 41. Daydream. 42. How would you solve it with an infinite budget? 43. Write out the problem with your opposite hand. 44. Sing the National Anthem with a cockney accent. 45. Eat dinner. 46. Change your brand of coffee. 47. Wash dishes. 48. Find the solution in the clouds. 49. Swing. 50. Take a nap at your desk. 51. Go bowling. 52. Spin in your chair shouting: "WHOOPEE!" 53. Eat a snow cone. 54. Contort your face in strange and unusual ways. 55. High-five yourself. 56. Go camping. 57. Take Spot for a walk. 58. Massage your scalp for 10 minutes. 59. Play musical chairs. 60. Go for a walk in the rain. 61. Pick up something with your toes. 62. Communicate. 63. Stand on your head. 64. Stand on someone else's head. 65. Go for a drive. 66. Call a psychic hotline, laugh at their predictions. 67. Caffeine. 68. More caffeine. 69. Imagine explaining the idea at an awards banquet. 70. Watch a TV show in another language. 71. Think about it before you go to sleep. 72. Call Mom, she can fix anything. 73. When in doubt, resort to duct tape. 74. Watch slasher movies to boost your creative confidence. 75. Fly a kite. 76. Shake up a can of pop and

open it. 77. Go for a walk. 78. Draw a picture of it. 79. Pretend to snorkel. 80. Think like a child. 81. Walk outside and wave to a stranger. 82. Look at the person's paper next to you. 83. Climb a tree. 84. Find a new word in the dictionary. 85. Make up your own word 86. Make a daisy chain. 87. Dance a polka. 88. Play in a toy store. 89. Just don't think about it. 90. Jump on a treadmill. 91. Alphabetize your refrigeratables. 92. Pretend like it doesn't matter. 93. Paint with your fingers. 94. Clean your toilet. 95. Lose yourself in your favorite music. 96. Watch old black & white reruns. 97. Listen to bees. 98. Walk in a grocery store—notice clever solutions. 99. Rake the leaves in your yard. 100. Sit outside and count the stars. 101. Still can't find the answer? **Bring in the Idea Monkeys!**

Order your very
own I Create mug.

Act now. Operators
are standing by.

Go to freetheideamonkey.com

(RING)LEADER To-Dos

Teach your team of Monkeys a variety of techniques that free their mind and let ideas flow (e.g., shower your way to creativity, sleep on it).

Open your team's stream of consciousness with a blank sheet of paper. This is not a metaphor. Swallow hard and demonstrate your ability to be open to new ideas.

Help them schedule their daydreaming around times that work best for their brain.

Make sure to laugh and have fun—if you're not having fun, you're doing it wrong!

Use success criteria to increase the likelihood of success. Rules should not limit the Monkey. They should challenge him.

QUICK! WRITE THE FIVE THINGS FOR WHICH YOU FEEL MOST GRATEFUL.

> _____
  _____
  _____

> _____
  _____
  _____

> _____
  _____
  _____

> _____
  _____
  _____

> _____
  _____
  _____

Chapter 8

The Upside of Problems

Surrounded on all sides? Attack!

Pop quiz, hot shot: what do MTV, Trader Joe's and the iPod have in common? Yes, of course, they're all now ubiquitous and make our lives much more agreeable.

But to me, the most interesting thing about all three is that they were born during recessions. (Trader Joe's: 1958; MTV: 1981; iPod: 2001, if you are scoring at home.)

And therein lies an important point. When you find yourself in tough times—the economy is heading downhill rapidly; your industry is suddenly plagued with problems—the last thing you want to do is retrench. If handled correctly, these "challenges" can be a good thing for your company. They can give you the opportunity—and the funds—to innovate and gain a substantial leg up on the competition.

> "My center is giving way, my right is pushed back, my left is wavering. The situation is excellent. I shall attack."
>
> Marshal Foch,
> Commander of the Allied Forces in World War I

But only if handled correctly.

That is never going to happen if your initial reaction to problems big (a recession) or small (you just received the resignation of a talented employee) is to say, "We have to tighten our proverbial belts; let's cut spending 22.73 percent across the board." People are going to be demoralized. And even worse, that is what most firms will be doing, and you're never going to gain a competitive edge doing the same thing as everyone else.

A CATALYST FOR INNOVATION

Cutting equally across the board is the coward's way of dealing with a problem. It assures that no one is going to yell—how could anyone possibly object to sharing the pain equally—and it gives the timid a built-in excuse to fail. ("Gee, I know no one liked our new product, but they slashed our budget 22.73 percent right before launch, so it wasn't my fault.")

> "Attacking is the only secret. Dare and the world always yields; or if it beats you sometimes, dare it again and it will succumb."
>
> William Makepeace Thackeray

But suppose you use the problem at hand not as an excuse or a reason for hiding under your desk, but rather as a catalyst for innovation? Instead of cutting everything by 22.73 percent, why not see the problem as a chance to whack 90 percent (or the whole darn thing) out of stuff that isn't working well?

Cutting off funding to your laggards would free up a lot of money to back the one, or possibly two, big ideas you have been working on—ideas that have a chance to become breakthrough products or services. If you want to be less aggressive, you could place more resources behind the existing ideas/programs/products that are already working well.

A TWO-PRONGED APPROACH

Two key assumptions are necessary to make this approach a successful reality. First, you should already have in place a solid strategy; one that has identified your company's competitive advantage so you know where to place your relatively big bets. (If you don't have a sound strategy, you are at a huge disadvantage.) And second, I am assuming—and I concede it is a huge assumption—that you have the intestinal fortitude to react to the problem at hand in a way that is not like everyone else.

> "Nobody ever defended anything successfully — there is only attack and attack and attack some more."
> General George S. Patton

If you are the chief executive officer, you can make this gutsy call on your own—assuming, of course, you get the board to go along. The rest of us probably need to take a two-pronged approach.

First, when the word comes down from on high that you need to belt-tighten, go through the usual drill. Explain that, instead of flying everyone in every three months for a meeting, you're going to make the meetings every four months instead—cutting that travel expense by 25 percent—and that you can probably get by with 12 people in the department as opposed to 13.

> It is well documented that brands that increase advertising during a recession when competitors are cutting back can improve market share and return on investment at lower cost than during good economic times.

But then go to your boss and say, "Instead of dealing with the need to cut like everyone else, why don't we use these hard times as an opportunity."

IMPORTANT!
Do not advertise unless you have first invented a differentiated product or service

You can talk, for example, about how now is exactly the right time to increase advertising. As Harvard Business School professor John A. Quelch noted, " ... outline how you plan to create an MTV, a Trader Joe's or an iPod of your own, complete with an aggressive launch timeline to ensure it is firmly established when the upheaval in the marketplace ends."

You can also point out that what you are advocating will leave your company perfectly positioned once the problem(s) end. While your competition is withdrawing, you will be charging ahead, taking market share.

Maybe neither argument will carry the day. But if it does nothing else, this kind of innovative thinking gives the boss another reason to keep you around.

You may have heard this story. Two shoe salesmen from the same company go to rural Asia in 1985. The first wires back this message: "situation bleek, nobody wears shoes." The second wires a different message: "Opportunities everywhere!!! Everybody needs shoes!!!" In times of challenge, the best (Ring)leaders know how to position aggressive ideas and the best Idea Monkeys know how to generate the ideas. And you guessed it, they sound just like the second shoe salesperson. Which one are you?

Almost all problems are temporary. Great companies and great Idea Monkeys (and the people who lead them) don't abandon their growth strategies in light of temporary setbacks. They attack  aggressively, while everyone else is pulling back.

In 1915, Walter Cannon published his seminal work on acute stress response. His theory boils down to this: all animals—including humans—have evolved to deal with stress in one of two ways: we stand and fight, or we run like crazy in the opposite direction. My advice? When it doubt, fight!

HOW TO CAPITALIZE ON HARD TIMES

Your competitors are likely to become much more conservative when times are tough. They'll cut budgets and limit (or eliminate) their innovation efforts to save cash.

In other words, they'll go out of their way to help you. It's like they are erecting a big flashing sign saying, "Please come and take some of our market share." Let us give you two ideas to help you capitalize on their weakness.

INNOVATION STRATEGY #1:
WIN IT NOW, EXPAND IT LATER

This is for the bravest among you. It gives you a chance to gain substantial market share. It works best if you are not under pressure to meet short-term financial hurdles.

If you are a privately held firm, your ears should have just perked up. And if you are part of a big, publicly traded firm, you should be very afraid. (As we will talk about later in Chapter 13, when it comes to innovation, David almost always beats Goliath. I know those of you who work for large firms don't want to hear it, but it is true.)

The win now, grow later strategy has little to do with short-term profit and everything to do with long-term growth. As we have seen, it has been well documented that maintaining marketing and innovation spending during market disruptions (recessions and the like) creates a major bounce once the market stabilizes, so if you gain market share during a downturn—even if it costs you money—your growth will be exponentially larger when the market recovers.

"My lemon is _____."

Here is a simple illustration from the most recent recession. In analyzing the marketing data, we saw that many mothers were buying baby formula at the beginning of the month, as soon as they got paid, because they were worried that they might run out of money sometime during the month.

Obviously, that was a bad sign for the economy. But it seemed to me to represent a huge opportunity for a company that already sells to new mothers to enter the market with a low-price baby formula.

If our mythical company provided an extremely high-quality product at a low cost during the recession, it would absolutely win share and loyalty from these worried moms. Profits would come later through economies of scale, the ability to reduce marketing costs once the brand was established; and, yes, the mothers' loyalty would help lift other products in the portfolio and probably support respectable price increases once the economy was on the mend.

STRATEGY #2: READY, AIM, AIM, AIM, FIRE

If you don't like, or can't implement Plan A (Win It Now, Expand It Later), then it is time for Plan B. If you have a disciplined research function, you are already sitting on insights into customer buying behaviors, segment value and marketing. (If you don't have it, start building it today.)

These insights enable you to build an innovation plan that lets you win one segment at a time, meaning you can lower your overall marketing budget, but still spend more than your competitors in certain segments and beat them soundly. The key is to keep or expand investments in specific areas of innovation that are sure fire.

An example would be Marriott. Each of its "brands" targets a particular segment: Marriott Suites for long-term vacationers; Residence Inn for extended stayers; and Courtyard for budget-conscious business travelers. (When faced with a recession, where do you think the company should focus innovation spending?)

The irony is that most innovation efforts fail because of lack of focus, i.e., budgets and teams are spread too thin. Our approach allows you to concentrate your brightest people and financial resources on "must win" innovation that will drive the majority of the growth during hard times.

LEAN INTO ADVERSITY AND FIND OPPORTUNITIES

When we talk about innovating during hard times, people immediately substitute "recession" for "hard times." And economic downturns certainly qualify as adversity. But adversity doesn't disappear when the economy is good. You can count on:

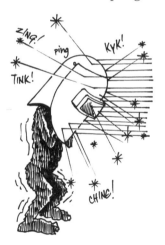

A. A competitor who does the unexpected and upends your market.

B. Consumers demanding something you just can't provide today.

C. Financing that you were absolutely certain was going to be there suddenly won't be.

When those things occur, conservative managers act as they always have: they slash marketing budgets. They hunker down and go the safe route. ("Hey, I know—instead of doing something daring, why don't we line extend our best product?")

Want to change history? Don't be one of those people. Stick to your growth strategy—ALWAYS.

Believe in yourself, and if you need inspiration to stay the course, borrow from the best. Warren Buffett made his fortune by following an adage he came up with a long time ago: "Be fearful when others are greedy—be greedy when others are fearful."

ANTICIPATE PROBLEMS: WAR GAMES

"What if I am missing something that is going to put me out of business?"

That question always ranks near the top when we ask CEOs to list their greatest fears. CEOs are increasingly asking us for the fastest way to create revolutionary change within their companies. Typically the request is rooted in their fear of being blindsided. The rapid pace of new technology has made leaders painfully aware that it is now possible for an upstart to change the rules of the game virtually overnight. Think Orbitz. Think Dyson. Think Craigslist. Think eBay. (If you believe that Sears was worried about eBay 20 years ago, you're forgetting that there was no such thing as eBay 20 years ago.)

Growing out of this worry of being made obsolete is a new trend in innovation: the use of war games. In the past, war games have been an internal exercise, usually a modification of the popular SWOT (strengths, weaknesses, opportunities, threats) analysis.

INNOVATION
✪WAR✪
GAMING

But what would happen if you paid a team of really smart people who knew virtually nothing about your industry to take an objective crack at building a product, service or business model that would rock (or even potentially destroy) your world? What if these people used a rigorous innovation process and had access to all your research and direct contact with every one of your department heads?

We call this Innovation War Gaming, and it is exactly what more and more CEOs are secretly doing today. Some hire consultants. Others literally hire entrepreneurs who have a track record of starting businesses. Some pay by the hour, some offer prizes, still others become shareholders of small firms *just* so they can be apprised of what's next. They realize that their biggest weakness is their own expertise. They understand that evolutionary ideas come from down their halls and revolutionary ideas will most certainly come from outside their walls.

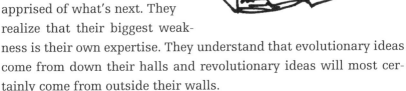

Worst case scenario: they sleep better at night because the innovation outsiders can't come up with anything that could destroy their business in the immediate future. Best case, they are presented with an industry-changing idea that they can launch or acquire if they choose.

(Ring)leader lessons from "The Art of War"

1. It is proper discipline that enables victories
2. Know Thy Enemy, Know Yourself
3. Measurement yields figures, which yield comparisons, which increase your chances of victory

WHAT IS YOUR BIGGEST BUSINESS CHALLENGE?

> _____

_____

_____

DESCRIBE THE BUSINESS OUTCOME YOU WANT.

> _____

_____

_____

WHAT STANDS IN THE WAY OF GETTING TO THIS OUTCOME?

> _____

_____

_____

> _____

_____

_____

> _____

_____

_____

(Great strategists use this formula as a starting point.)

(RING)LEADER To-Dos

Worry before you need to worry. Have your Monkeys try to put you out of business before your industry/competitor does. You want to find your blind spots before the competition does.

When in doubt, fight! Stick to your growth strategy.

Remember, differentiation is the ultimate profit weapon. Monkeys are masters at imagining the unique products and services that your customers want.

WHAT IS A BIG MISTAKE YOU'VE MADE IN LIFE?

> _____

_____

_____

_____

_____

NOW, WHAT WAS THE BAD ASSUMPTION YOU MADE THAT LED TO THE MISTAKE?

> _____

_____

_____

_____

_____

(Insights are like assumptions. Get them right and life is easier.)

Chapter 9

Ignorance is Bliss.
It is Also Expensive.
The Art and Science of Being Insightful

"Colonel Mustard did it in the library with a wrench," yelled my older brother Bill. "He took out Professor Plum because Plum had stolen the Mustard family's secret recipe for grilled cheese and sold it to Kraft, depriving Mustard of millions."

And so ended another game of Clue at the Maddock home. In my family, getting to make up the "why" behind the murder in the board game was the real prize. Anyone could figure out the culprit, but he who could create the most compelling hypothesis about the motive was the true champion (despite what the official rules of the game may have said).

When you look at leading innovators, you quickly realize the most important ingredient by far is the story behind the game—the market insight that led to their success. And unfortunately, when it comes to what customers really value, too many of us just don't have a Clue.

Here's an unfortunate case in point. Ten years ago, we were hired by Enesco to help them with a new product line called Creatures of Delight®. At the time, Enesco sold popular items including Precious Moments™, those cute little ceramic figurines that your grandma collects. And Enesco sure knew how to sell them. Unfortunately, when they called us, we were told sales were slowing and they needed a new idea.

Enesco was really good at selling ceramics to moms and grandmas and told us they wanted to sell something that would appeal to their kids and grandkids. At the time, a favorite idea was the Creatures of Delight® line. The Creatures were deliberately hideous. They were brightly colored monsters, something that you might expect to find living under a log just east of Oz. Really creepy. But we thought, who knows? This might be just the kind of thing that kids might like. They buy Pokémon, right?

Get A Clue.
Collect the **facts.**
Ask **why,**
identify the **frictions...**
then
make your move!

What made the idea incredibly interesting to us was an insight that Enesco uncovered. They found that kids love to build relationships through learning and exploring, but their new playground—the Internet—at the time offered few appropriate options. Enesco thought that these crazy creatures should have their own Internet world made just for kids. Their idea was to sell the creatures with a code so that kids could go online and unlock "Creature rooms" using their code, play fun games and discover more about their creature friends. This, in theory, would make them want to buy more creatures.

Brilliant right? To us, it sounded like they were on to something.*

So we went about the work of creating the fantasyland that these Creatures would live in, full of techno-color landscapes, secret passageways and games. We wrote descriptions of each Creature's likes and dislikes and tried to give each its own special personality.

*Note: They *were* on to something. Just look at the success of Webkinz™ a few years later.

I am now tired of writing about this story because I know how it ends. (And you have already guessed.) The project was a failure. Why? We did not have a clear understanding of the insight(s) that would drive moms and kids to buy the product. In fact, we failed in multiple ways.

1. We thought Enesco had hit on the big idea when they told us about how kids wanted to build deeper relationships with these dolls. When we asked about how much research they had done to prove the point, they had assured us they had done "enough." Unfortunately, they hadn't. We should have pushed for a deeper understanding of the consumers' needs and wishes.

2. But that could have been okay if our second assumption had been right. We thought Enesco had the clout to drive this new line through retail partners. If so, we may have been able to do some learning in market. I have no idea what happened here. We were not part of this conversation. Perhaps the buyer didn't like the product or maybe the sales were light at launch.

At the time, we lacked the experience or the authority to demand more learning at the onset of the project and to drive the proper dialogue. Today we would have quickly realized that our assumptions, and some of their insights, were incomplete, and done something about it. Ignorance may be bliss. But it's also expensive.

Insights are the heart of innovation. Without them, you will not have a clue what your consumers/customers want/need. Without knowing what they want/need, any idea you come up with will be just a guess at best.

What is an insight? An insight is a penetrating consumer (customer) truth that helps you build your business. Penetrating in that it is true for a large group of people; the problem to solve is so big that the large group of people will flock to your product or service once you solve it.

Finding that insight isn't easy—but it is vital. Let me give you another example that proves getting the insight right is fundamental to innovation success and how, sometimes, a single insight can drive your business for decades.

About ten years ago, Doug Harrison, founder of the Scooter Store agreed to speak to a small group of my entrepreneurial friends in Florida. The Scooter Store sells power chairs — some indeed, look like scooters, others are motorized wheelchairs — to elderly and disabled people, and Doug had managed to create a meteoric rise in revenue since he founded the company in 1991.

As a marketer who was very aware of the fact that Baby Boomers are well on their way to becoming a huge senior citizen cohort, I was keen to understand what he knew about aging boomers.

Just before attending Doug's speech, I did some research on boomers. I speculated that there were a number of insight nuggets that could be behind Doug's success. Below are a few of my guesses.

A. Boomers felt underserved and Doug had created an empathetic culture and story that made them feel comfortable and understood.
B. The Scooters were a better technology. Maybe they were hipper. Maybe they were faster. Maybe they were easier to use.
C. The process for buying a scooter was complicated and scary, and Doug had found a way to simplify it, perhaps by limiting the models available or having an extremely well-trained sales staff.
D. Wheelchairs meant old. Perhaps changing the language to scooters made people feel younger.
E. The Scooters were priced correctly.

OK, stop for a second. Read the previous list again and see how good you are at this; which one of my guesses was right?

The fact is, all my answers were right — sort of. But if I had gone into the Scooter business based on any *or even all* of these "insights" governing how I positioned my Scooter business, I would have lost my shirt. I had a bunch of what I considered solid, educated guesses and I was able to get pretty close to the answer, but as the cliché goes, close only works when you are playing horseshoes or throwing hand grenades. In business, close is too often another word for "pending bankruptcy."

Now think. The last time you started an innovation initiative, didn't you come to the table with solid, educated guesses? Didn't smart people within your organization talk about an ingredient or technology that you had that was clearly superior to the competition? Wasn't there a feeling in the room that the collective experience was enough to figure out the challenge without doing a whole bunch of research? Didn't *you* think that you had it figured out? In this case, I did—and I was wrong.

In this case, my insights were right, but they were insufficient (in addition to being obvious). Of course, seniors feel confined and want to get out and do things; of course, seniors want easy technology; of course, seniors don't want to feel like a burden ... but all those things completely missed the one insight that has been the driving force behind the Scooter Store's success for the last two decades. If you see their ads on TV today, you still hear this version of the promise that uses Doug's key insight as its marketing hook: "If we approve you for a Scooter and Medicare refuses to pay for it, we'll give it to you for free—guaranteed."

It turns out that the key insight was that seniors wanted scooters because they wanted more free-dom, but they were afraid they couldn't afford them. Doug learned the most important insight for his business: if that fear was alleviated, if insurance would cover the cost, they would buy in a heartbeat.

This one insight became fundamental to Doug's business model, his marketing, his compensation plan—everything. He trained his team to literally become Medicare experts. By being able to work through bureaucratic hurdles, they took away the biggest obstacle to purchasing. To their customers, it seemed that Doug's people often knew the Medicare process better than the people did at Medicare. He was able to make and keep the promise that mattered to his customers and sales went through the roof.

Here's the point: your team will be faced with hundreds of insights, any one of which could be the cornerstone of a successful launch. Get it right and you win; miss and you lose. If you choose to trust your gut, the likelihood of being correct is incredibly low. I believe that the mistake of trusting your instinct is one of the biggest reasons for innovation failure. Think about that the next time you are relying on your years of industry experience to make the "right" call.

INSIGHTS: A SIMPLE EQUATION

Put simply, an insight is an understanding that helps solve a problem. I tend to think about it this way:

Fact + Reason Why + Friction = Insight

Example: my boss needs insights because he wants us to be successful at innovation, but he wouldn't recognize a good one if it bit him in the butt.

So, what you are looking for is a need and some sort of friction that keeps that need from being met. Here's an example:

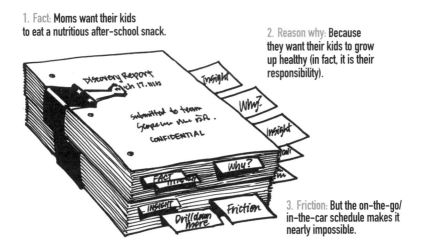

1. Fact: **Moms want their kids to eat a nutritious after-school snack.**

2. Reason why: **Because they want their kids to grow up healthy (in fact, it is their responsibility).**

3. Friction: **But the on-the-go/in-the-car schedule makes it nearly impossible.**

Are the ideas starting to pop into your mind?

The "but" statement (... but their kids are super busy and always at an activity or in the car) points out the friction that we're trying to solve. It is what drives the ideas. The more people who have this problem, the bigger the opportunity for your company. This is just one insight—there are potentially hundreds more.

THE PLATFORM STATEMENT

Think of a platform as a bucket that you can put a lot of insights into. Creating a platform is a simple process of coming up with a lot of insights and looking for common themes that allow you to ladder up to larger and more compelling insight platforms.

The platform of "I want my kids to eat a nutritious after-school snack because it is my responsibility to help them grow up healthy, but the on-the-go/in-the-car schedules make it nearly impossible" was made up of a lot of other insights. Here are a few:

- My kids are always on the go because they have lots of activities, but they don't eat right as a result.
- I want my kids to have enough fuel so they enjoy their extra-curricular activities because I want them to be happy, but it is hard to make sure they eat right.
- I worry about my kids' health because their active lifestyles don't allow for good eating habits, but there are not many nutritious foods they can eat on the go.
- I feel guilty feeding my kids junk food between activities because their health is important to me, but fast food is the most convenient option.

Remember: An insight is a penetrating consumer (customer) truth that helps you build your business. Penetrating in that it is true for a large group of people, and business building in that there is a big problem to solve so that the large group of people will flock to your product or service.

Here's a good test. Once you have collected insights and linked them to a larger opportunity platform, see if people start giving you ideas to solve your challenge. In this case, they will likely start inventing things like a sandwich wrap, a granola bar, a frozen banana, a veggie panini stick, a pretzel rod filled with cream cheese. Many years ago a similar exercise resulted in handheld food for McDonald's, which included what is today the Snack Wrap. It is nice to have worked on my very favorite fast food.

INTUITION ISN'T ENOUGH

"What if I am wrong?" This phrase, often whispered from the darkest corners of the subconscious, keeps otherwise brilliant people from changing the world.

The very thought that an idea may fail is usually enough to create the internal inertia that keeps it from happening; you move more slowly, you invest less, you don't fight for the idea quite as hard.

If you think you will succeed, or think you will fail, you are correct.
— Henry Ford

Conversely, Idea Monkeys often charge through life without these murmurs of doubt, so getting them to do the right kind of research (See "Great Insights Start With Great Questions" later in the chapter) may be your challenge. While their coworkers are paralyzed by fear and doubt, they are screaming "damn the torpedoes" and moving full-steam ahead.

And this, sadly, is where they often hit an iceberg.

There are two simple solutions for this challenge. The first involves self-awareness. If you know that you—or the Idea Monkey you manage—always err on the side of optimism, then make sure you have a Yin for your (his) Yang (see Chapter 12); someone who can objectively and respectively challenge that enthusiasm.

The second solution is simply to stop and prove you are working on an insight worthy of your brilliance.

That would have saved Motorola millions. In the 1990s, Motorola mortgaged much of their future on Iridium, a phone system capable of keeping everyone—including people climbing Mount Everest—connected. The system, which reportedly relied on 66 separate satellites orbiting the earth, was an incredibly complex and we believe ridiculously expensive undertaking.

What makes this failure so utterly unbelievable is that it seems if Motorola had stopped to measure the power of their insight, they would have found out that there are only 150 people who climb Everest each year. And even if you assume the market for people who absolutely, positively need to be able to make a call no matter where they are in the known universe at any given point, you only have a market of say, 1,322. That simply was not going to support Motorola's investment.

But it did not matter.

The Idea Monkeys at Motorola, in this case brilliant technologists and thought leaders, were apparently so enamored with the satellite-driven technology that there was just no stopping them ... unfortunately for Motorola's shareholders.

GREAT INSIGHTS START WITH GREAT QUESTIONS

There are seven key questions you want to ask to discover a key insight: Who? What? When? Where? Why? How? And finally, how many?

Dig deeper and you can build a list of hundreds of questions that naturally fall out of these seven from a client, consumer and customer perspective. These questions may include:

- What are the consumers'/customers' current behaviors?
- What are the consumers' needs (met and unmet, articulated and unarticulated)?
- How are consumers solving current challenges?
- When, where and why do they do what they do to solve these challenges?
- Who are they doing it with?

Who? What? When? Where? Why? How? And ... how many?

FRESH PERSPECTIVE

The opportunity for trying to discover the key insight from multiple angles is available to researchers, too.

In 2007, we acquired Markitecture, a research firm focused on innovation. The partners at the firm had come from the nation's best business schools and been trained at some of the most respected research firms in the country before heading off to start their own company. They were masters at classic quantitative and qualitative research methodologies like segmentation, conjoint, store intercepts, online surveys, etc. It was clear that they were a bunch of very skilled, very bright people.

But after working on a project or account for awhile, they eventually shared many of the same biases as their clients; they knew too much about an industry to see things objectively. So they naturally interpreted data the same way their clients did. (See our discussion on stuck inside the jar in Chapter 4.)

After buying Markitecture, we got together with the partners and asked, "What are we missing in this research and how do we see it again?" In other words, we asked how can we gain different perspectives in finding key insights for our clients. It is a very important question.

The answer led us to develop dozens of research methodologies in which we intentionally infused the perspective of outside experts to reinterpret the data, and uncover insights that we were missing. We found, to our initial surprise, that *every* research method was enhanced through fresh perspective.

Why?

Anyone who has walked through a field with a young child knows that they can make you aware of the smallest details that you have not noticed in years—the angles on a blade of grass; the insects on the bottom of a rock; the sounds of crickets. Look at this illustration: quickly jot down what it could be.

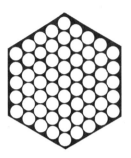

Here's what a few of our folks came up with inside of 15 minutes:

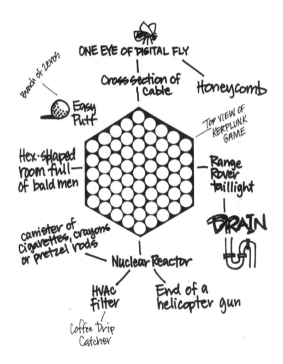

Just like any idea, a brilliant insight is one that makes the connections that others miss. Your job managing Monkeys is to allow them to apply their wonder(full) lens to as many challenges as possible. Your job as the Idea Monkey is to uncover as many possibilities as possible.

So the secret of great research is simple: generate as many insights as possible by having your particular opportunity interpreted by brilliant people who can be objective and creative about what they are seeing. The right combination of methodology and expertise will yield a powerful insight every time. Conversely, using traditional methods, interpreted by the same people, will usually yield little or no new information.

QUANTIFY THE INSIGHT FIRST

Necessity is the mother of invention. It is also the evil godmother of blown budgets, broken hearts and shattered careers. I'm not being overly dramatic. I've seen it and it ain't pretty.

The next time you think you have identified a meaningful need in the market, do yourself a favor: make sure you know how big it is. For the inventor or entrepreneur, this means brewing a pot of coffee and sitting down with your new buddy, Google, for a day or two. Research how many people represent your target, how much money they spend in the category, how fast the category is growing or shrinking, how many other products meet the need, how much they cost, and where they buy the products.

Strive to collect as many quantitative data points as possible. If you work hard, this deep dive into secondary research will help you prioritize which insights are the most powerful and which don't pass muster.

Then, if humanly (and financially possible), use primary research—surveys, focus groups, and the like—to confirm which insight provides the biggest market opportunity.

RESEARCHERS DEBUNKED

For many years, I was afraid to meet with researchers. I saw them as people who stood in the way of my desire to create ideas. The truth is, I've had one too many fastballs thrown my way by a researcher bully who wanted to strut their stuff by citing some obscure data point. Research bullies are bad people and I suggest you avoid them at all costs.

But in my heart, I've always been fascinated by human behavior and psychology—two drivers of great research. I love understanding how people's fears and desires drive them to behave around products and services. Great researchers are curious people who know how to use tools. They are people who can remain objective and see things that others miss. And, as my experience with the bullies shows, they are incredibly rare.

BRING IN AN OUTSIDER

Javier Flaim, expert researcher and partner at Maddock Douglas, has come to believe that infusing outside perspective in even the most traditional research methodologies (one example: focus groups) is one of the simplest ways for any company to get from average insights to breakthrough insights.

Javi is a smart guy. Here's how it could work. Simply invite an outsider—someone smart who knows nothing about the business idea being tested—to sit in and observe the focus group—and listen to what they take away from the session. Remember: Idea Monkey's see things differently. Let them.

Surround yourself with curious experts

| IGNORANCE IS BLISS. IT IS ALSO EXPENSIVE.

SOMETIMES TO SUCCEED, YOU NEED TO BE PLAYING FOR A DIFFERENT TEAM

Are you stuck? Some companies are built to discover new insights, some are not. See if this resonates:

"Stuck" Company Insight

I want great insights because I know they lead to meaningful innovation and profits, but I am stuck in an organization that keeps doing new product development the same way.

Meanwhile, we see aggressive innovators at smaller companies dealing with a different kind of struggle. The insight that applies to them usually sounds something like this:

We want great new products because we need to be distinctly different than our huge competitor, but we have limited resources and need to move really fast (so we are going to have to be creative and challenge convention …).

From our experience, if you really want to make a difference in the world, your best bet is on a company with an entrepreneurial mind-set. The irony is that every year, undercapitalized companies put giant businesses on their heels simply because they are willing to dig, discover and capitalize on insights that are readily available to everyone.

As I'll talk about later, David usually beats Goliath. If you are stuck, I recommend you move your big brain to a company that fails forward and starts with an entrepreneurial mind-set. Losing money is one thing. Losing your inventive soul is too high a price to pay for anything.

NAME THREE NEEDS IN YOUR LIFE OR BUSINESS THAT YOU SEE SHIFTING.

> _____

> _____

> _____

NOW, WHAT CAN YOU CREATE TO ADDRESS THESE NEEDS?

> _____

> _____

> _____

IGNORANCE IS BLISS. IT IS ALSO EXPENSIVE.

(RING)LEADER To-Dos

Bring in outsiders to help with insights. Monkeys thrive in every industry.

Flip the way you do things. Instead of settling for intuitive/"right enough" insights, collect all the facts, identify the friction, and *then* (and only then) do you make your move.

Confirm that the insight is true for a large group of people, i.e., quantify the insights.

Doodle time. Study after study shows that if you give your brain a break, it will surprise you with a big idea.

IGNORANCE IS BLISS. IT IS ALSO EXPENSIVE.

Chapter 10
Social Media: Now and Forever

Idea Monkeys often embrace technology and new concepts ahead of everyone else. We need to catch up with them. That's especially true when it comes to new media.

At Maddock Douglas, we believe this with all our hearts: while social media is complex and often misunderstood, it has value beyond traditional marketing. More specifically, we believe it can be used to help form your marketing strategy and should be integrated into all your communications, allowing your Idea Monkeys to succeed faster and have far greater impact.

SOCIAL MEDIA AS AN INNOVATION TOOL

While many have been collecting friends on Facebook and followers on Twitter, we've been enthusiastically watching social media's rise as an effective innovation tool. Innovation is about ideas and communication. Online communities are often a perfect place to find and test insights. Online influencers are redefining the focus group. Best yet, when your online influencers help you create new products, services or business models, they become instant ambassadors of your brand, creating the spark effect that eludes so many companies. People support what they create.

It gets better: the emergence of social media tracking tools give researchers and marketers alike a bevy of instant information to optimize targeting, messaging and new product ideas. If you are a left-brained innovator, life is good. If you are not taking advantage of social media, you are missing an opportunity to create and launch better ideas faster.

We have invested heavily in social media at our company. We believe in the power of online communities to help uncover insights; generate and validate new products, services and business models; and most important, create the necessary conversations that spark a new idea we can develop and introduce across the globe.

Everything it has done for us, we believe it can do for your organization as well.

Our research shows that marketers intend to invest more in social media in the years ahead, but they have yet to allot substantial budgets to it. That isn't the way to go. And if you fund social applications only as experiments, you're unlikely to be able to make an impact.

OWNERSHIP IS FLEETING

The purpose with this chapter is twofold.

First, let's clarify exactly what we (and you) should be talking about when using the term "social media," and then we will address the three biggest worries about implementing it:

- the loss of control,
- the related concern that someone in your employ will make a mistake during real-time interactions with customers, and perhaps the biggest misconception of all,
- that there is no way to measure its impact.

Simple definition first: social media are a technically enhanced —think Internet and mobile-based—way of discussing ideas with people in communities. (Twitter, blogs, both niche communities and giant communities like LinkedIn and Facebook are the sorts of things we are talking about here.) Social media use words, pictures, audio and video to foster interaction.

It is that interaction that makes some business people nervous. We understand.

When you advertise in a publication or on radio or TV or even the Internet, you decide on the words, the imagery and everything else. When you use social media to get that message out, that ownership is fleeting. While you maintain absolute control over the initial content, what happens afterward depends on the audience. Is there any way to alter that? No.

But instead of worrying about it, we think you should see it as an opportunity—one that you already have some (analogous) experience with.

"To swear off making mistakes is very easy. All you have to do is swear off having ideas."
—Leo Burnett

TIGHTLY VS. LOOSELY SCRIPTED

Many companies have call centers—places where they handle orders and provide customer service over the phone. The people in those centers are trained and given various "scripts" to follow, but no interaction with a customer (or potential customer) goes exactly as the company has drawn it up.

Still, just about every company finds call centers an effective way to maintain service levels and boost sales. Why should social media be any different?

"But suppose employees make a mistake and say or promise something they shouldn't during these interactions?" we're often asked.

The answer to that is simple: You handle it exactly the way you would any other mistake or problem. You fix it and put steps in place to minimize the chances it will happen again. And if you use that worry as an excuse for not engaging in social media, you are putting yourself at a huge disadvantage.

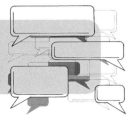

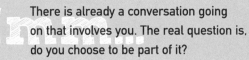
There is already a conversation going on that involves you. The real question is, do you choose to be part of it?

Raff recently addressed a national association of hotel executives, and one person, a vice president at a huge chain, raised the "what-if-a-customer-writes-something-bad-about-us?" issue during the Q + A.

He listened patiently and then hit him with some research he'd done about his company in preparation for the meeting.

"I did a Google search about weddings held at the biggest hotel in your region," he said. "And while I found all the wonderful pictures you posted about the facility on your website, I also found troubling items that came up on wedding-related blogs—in particular, two women who went on at great length about the problems they had with their receptions at this hotel. There was no response from the hotel anywhere."

"The posts were three years old. What kind of impact do you think the comments by those women are going to have on someone looking for a place to have their wedding?"

His point was if the company had been monitoring mentions of its hotels on social media, it could have responded to the complaints for all the world to see. Instead, the company missed its chance to redeem itself and probably cost itself revenue. Even if only one potential customer was scared off after reading those negative blog comments, it was too many.

"Did you hear about Ruthiesgarden.com?"

MEASURABLE RETURN

As for the last objection, that there is no way to measure the impact social media have on revenues and profits: that is just wrong. A quick Google search on measuring social media turns up over seven million hits. A more in-depth search finds over 120 tools that have been developed to do the same. A still deeper search reveals this: we're gaining on it. Tools and metrics are becoming more accurate even as new social media platforms arise.

In every circle there are influencers. These people are the Holy Grail of advertising. Social Media finally gives us a way to find them, learn from them, respond to them, and let them inspire their circle. What we have always dreamed of is now possible. *—Smart Person*

(Ironically, if we probe deeper, invariably the executives suggesting that social media impact is not measurable don't have many metrics or ROI in place with most of their other marketing efforts either. Our point here: you should align all your marketing with key financial outcomes/objectives and measure it in the context of those objectives.)

But knowing you can measure the bang you get for the buck is not the end point when it comes to social media. The real question to ask is: "Are we getting what we want out of the conversation?" Without focusing on measurable objectives, it's difficult to justify further investment. Or as the philosopher George Harrison put it: "If you don't know where you are going, any road will take you there."

Then again, just because you can measure something doesn't mean it matters. Sure, you can discover that 436,315 young women have commented on your blog about the latest in skin care, but if that activity isn't moving the sales needle, it isn't helping you. The only metrics that matter are the ones that support your objectives. (Typical goals include increased brand awareness, increased sales, accelerated new product adoption, enhanced organic search ranking/visibility, customer retention and real-time insight.)

Now, these metrics don't exist in a vacuum. Your competition will be using social media as well, so you want to be smart about which you use. If you want something important to measure, gauge where you stand vis-à-vis with the competition. See who has the advantage based on positive/negative brand perceptions, organic search-term content/ranking, visibility and their observable overall social strategy.

If you haven't found a way to measure social media yet, you haven't looked hard enough.

We have two suggestions about how to do it. First, identify the key social media most used by your customers, and then evaluate their choices by not only popularity but also how believable they think they are.

FIND OUT WHERE THE TRUST IS

Nicholas Kinports, founder of ADMAVEN and our MD business partner, has a wonderful way of thinking about implementing your social media strategy. "It isn't about making content go viral—though that would be a wonderful by-product should it happen—or creating the next great Facebook application," Kinports says. "It's about structuring, and in some cases restructuring, how a business views and interacts with its customer base. The modern consumer is savvy, aware and fully able to make informed decisions, thanks to a wealth of information freely available on the Internet. The consumer of the near future will make purchase decisions based on information gleaned from unbiased peers and influencers. Social media is the latest tool through which these interactions occur."

Paraphrasing Nick, you can't out-clever your customer. It is best to see the world as they do and discover where they are going for trusted advice and then, and only then, interact in an honest, genuine way. You need to become a welcomed, trusted consultant.

If you think of social media as that—a social consultant—the results can be remarkable from both a bottom line and competitive standpoint. But to be in the game, you first need the desire to be social—and the strategy to do it authentically. There's a big difference between a company that behaves like a dabbler and one that behaves like a master when it comes to social media.

Where does your company fall?

THE IDEA MONKEY FOR PRESIDENT!

Idea Monkeys can thrive anywhere—even in political organizations. For example, Chris Hughes, director of online organizing, masterfully used social media to coordinate community support and action that ultimately led to Barack Obama's election as the 44th president of the United States.

Even while virtually every expert was predicting a Clinton (Hillary, in this case) win in the Democratic primary, Obama himself embraced social media as a lever that would change the rules of the game.

The results? More than three million Facebook friends, 200,000+ offline events, 35,000 Obama-related groups, 400,000+ blogs and nearly 15 million viewing hours on YouTube. The MyBarackObama.com site raised more than $500 million through average donations of under $100, while also being a strong catalyst for getting young people to register to vote.

No stakes are higher than those in U.S. politics, so why didn't any other candidate employ social media so effectively?

People close to Obama will tell you that the principle of "ideas from anywhere" is central to his leadership style. This precept, although democratic (a small "d" in this case), is not the way the political machine in the U.S. works, and a radical idea like social media as a campaign device was unlikely to survive the internal voting process—it took a maverick to make it happen.

Lesson: you cannot control the conversation, but you can certainly win being part of it.

TRUTH OR DARE (MONKEY STYLE)

I dare you (CMO, brand manager, PR communications specialist, CRM manager or whoever you are) to have your company authentically enter into the innovative realm of online social media, the world of Facebook and other networking sites (or as it was briefly known in shorthand, Web 2.0).

Not ready yet? Afraid you won't have control of what happens? C'mon, I double dare you.

Still not that daring? OK. If you won't take the dare, you have to tell the truth. Is your company customer focused?

"Yes, of course" (you answer without thinking). Seriously now, be honest. Does your institution really care about its customers or only about itself?

"Our customers," you reply.

I believe you. But what I believe doesn't matter. And the fact is, survey after survey says your customers don't believe you.

The reason is obvious. Your organization is seen as a corporation, and corporations in the eyes of most people are evil. Large companies—with a 13 percent approval rating—rank just above Congress and law firms when people are asked to list the most admired institutions in America, according to Harris Interactive.

In fact, if people were to anthropomorphize your organization, your firm would be seen as highly antisocial at best and psychopathic at worst. Yikes!

REVERSE THE ANTICORPORATE SLANT

The impassioned polemic, otherwise known as the movie *The Corporation*, asked people to describe big business.

Among their answers:

- "Self-interested"
- "Inherently amoral"
- "Callous and deceitful"
- "It breaches social and legal standards to get its way"
- "It does not suffer guilt"

Yes, the movie has an anticorporate slant. But Harris Interactive chose its people at random and companies would not have scored at the bottom of the pack if those surveyed thought of workplaces in the same light as Mother Teresa.

So this is what you are up against. People think companies are inherently bad. It's no wonder they don't believe you when you say you are customer-centric, no matter how many times you profess you are.

21ST CENTURY RESPONSIBILITY

But you can change that. The 21st century, with wikis, blogs and the millions of niche online communities, etc., allows us to create a more level playing field when it comes to customer relationships. It's now possible for us to share with consumers what we as companies are really all about and what we believe, face-to-face, so to speak.

That's a big responsibility. Is your company up to it?

The bad news is you can't hide from these innovations. They are now part of the daily fabric of most of your customers' lives. Even more bad news: if you're opting out, by default, your absence will brand you as antisocial and insincere when it comes to being customer-centric.

The good news is that the innovative technology you need to use is the easy part. The better news is if your intentions are authentic, your marketing budget is certain to experience exponential efficiency with infinite potential. And the best news is that social media is a wonderful new stage for Idea Monkeys guided by skillful (Ring)leaders. People have always responded to creativity. The "life of the party" gets the most attention. When these people are also genuine and respected, they are capable of movements that change history. Companies are just beginning to dabble with social media. Imagine what is going to happen when they put their most creative leaders on the case.

MASTERING SOCIAL NETWORKING

So what are the fundamentals you need to master in this new world? There are three.

Phase 1: Create the proper presence. First, you need to identify where your target is and which communities are important to them. You want to be where your customers, and potential customers, hang out. Having identified those places, you need to understand the conventions and etiquette of those environments. Every site is different, but if you keep the following in mind, you won't go too far astray. Do figure out ways to foster, nurture and support the community you are interacting with. Don't even think about a hard sell. Think about it. Your friends don't sell you on ideas. They don't need to. You trust them. If they started to sell you on something, they would likely begin to lose your trust.

Phase 2: Gain credibility based on your target's world view. The information you enter in the social media arenas must be carefully selected and composed with that environment in mind. Your message and content need to be all about them and what you can do to make their lives better. This means: "Help Them, Don't Sell Them." Be unconditionally generous. Visit Nike.com, one example of a company that does this well, to see what it's done for runners.

If we are adequately entertaining and educating customers, they will seize the opportunity to fully engage. They will share this content and perhaps even build on it—whether you invite them to or not—because that's what social beings do.

Speaking of the future …

Close your eyes and dream with us.

What if R&D, marketing, finance, planning, account services and creative all got together for a day and were capable of birthing an idea? What some companies call departments and partners are too often silos—emblems of inefficiency.

Cross-functional, open teams are the key to driving industry-changing products, services and new business models to market. This is true whether you work in a big company or a small one.

To ensure that silos are not an issue, some companies are even putting these blended teams in another building—an Innovation Center—and saying, "You have one year to change our world—go!"

More than a decade ago we moved to an "open" innovation model that enrolled leaders from each division *and* outside experts from around the globe. Today, being "social" and being innovative are one and the same.

When engagement reaches this level of mutual involvement, we move into the third phase:

Phase 3: Co-creating dialogue (The place where your company reaps the benefit of exchange.) Once we have defined and built the right presence, along with crafting the appropriate, engaging content, we can begin fostering true exchange of ideas and emotions.

This is where your best ideas can shine. We can create promotions, campaigns and conversations based on user-generated content, and empower our customers to not just be a part of our story, but to erase the line between "us" and "them."

It's important for your company to support a presence in social media. These new communities are irrevocably changing the landscape for marketers and how we communicate and innovate. Increasingly we are being charged with delivering ideas that engage and influence the people in these living, breathing and highly responsive human communities. This presents both a unique challenge and opportunity: we need to integrate our message and presence effectively, profitably and appropriately into social media communities. The presence you build within social media will be analyzed, scrutinized and perhaps criticized. However, entering this territory—which is controlled by the digital swarms of consumers and their communities—with the right voice and then nurturing that conversation in a manner authentic to your brand, your products and your customer will ultimately have a far greater positive impact on your level of opportunity over the existing risks. In fact, the greatest risk is being absent from that conversation—while your competition gains a powerful foothold.

(RING)LEADER To-Dos

Take advantage of social media to find and test insights, validate new ideas and create the necessary conversations to accelerate the new product adoption curve.

Be authentic, honest, genuine (and yes, be strong enough to be vulnerable). You cannot control the conversation, but you can win by being a part of it.

Create the proper presence; gain credibility based on your target's world view; co-create the dialogue.

Make sure you know what you want to get out of the conversation and then make sure you're getting it (measure effectively).

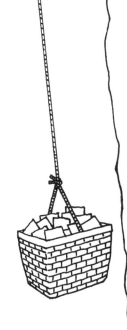

NAME THREE PARTNERS, PEOPLE OR COMPANIES THAT COULD HELP TRIPLE YOUR BUSINESS.

> _____
>
> _____
>
> _____

> _____
>
> _____
>
> _____

> _____
>
> _____
>
> _____

(Now, go meet with them and co-create a big idea.)

Chapter 11

Change Your Perspective,
Change the World

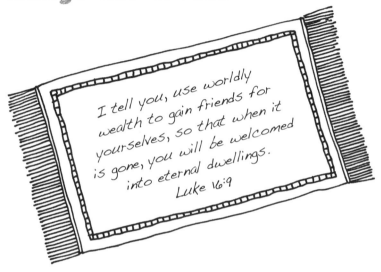

I tell you, use worldly wealth to gain friends for yourselves, so that when it is gone, you will be welcomed into eternal dwellings.

Luke 16:9

In 2008, Oprah Winfrey created a short-lived reality series called *The Big Give*. The premise was pretty simple. Each week, a small group of people—chosen for their dynamic personalities—was plopped into a town and challenged to be more creatively generous with a small amount of money than the next team. At the end of each episode, the person who did the least with the resources to benefit others was eliminated. This usually happened as I sat crying like a little girl in my living room. At season's end, the most creative giver was named the winner. The show was kind of like *The Apprentice* with more heart—which is to say that Donald Trump still hasn't made me cry.

Every episode was different. Sometimes Oprah would give the teams money, sometimes not. Sometimes she would point them to a particular need, e.g., a school, a family, a hospital. In other episodes she would have them find their own causes. Winning contestants were selected by how creatively they brought joy into people's lives and who did more with less. Despite my crying episodes, I absolutely loved the show.

The show reminded me of the biblical parable of the talents. As the story goes, a master gives three servants money (talents) before he leaves on a trip. The servant given five talents invests aggressively and doubles his master's money. The servant given two talents does the same. But the third servant, given only one talent, buries his for fear he will blow the opportunity. The master calls both of the aggressive investors "my good and faithful servants" and rewards them with more responsibility. In what seems to be a bit of biblical irony, he gets extremely angry at the guy who took no risks with his and calls him "a wicked and slothful servant." Ouch.

This parable and Oprah's show really spoke to me as a business owner. Even though I was usually too busy drawing caricatures of nuns to pay much attention in religious ed class, I am pretty certain that this parable supports the idea of entrepreneurial investing and conscious capitalism; i.e., to whom much is given, much is required. (I also think that if you follow the parallel, in her show, Oprah was playing God. But I digress.)

The runner-up winner on *The Big Give* was Cameron Johnson. I've had the pleasure of spending time with Cameron and he is the classic entrepreneur. He went from selling a few of his sister's old toys online—at nine years old—to being one of the top online Beanie Babies distributors, someone with a net worth of a million dollars before he was old enough to have a checking account. On the show, Cameron had no problem picking up the phone and letting his network in on the fun of helping people out. He aggressively sold the idea of doing good and his methods were creative and unconventional. In one episode, he randomly stopped by an auto repair shop and bailed out customers having trouble paying to get their cars fixed. He reasoned that people need to drive to be productive. He, like many young people today, are onto an idea that is changing the world:

you can do well by doing good. Business has much to learn from the newest breed of Idea Monkeys.

But too often the people with the best intentions get in their own way. For example, if the social responsibility movement spent less time hectoring and more time pointing out the greater profits companies can produce by implementing their ideas, they would be more effective.

This is not about saying "no" to profits. It is about recasting the issue in terms of "and," as in "you can do X, which will increase earnings **and** (by the way) contribute to the greater good," instead of "or," as in "you can do well **or** make money, you can't do both." The next generation of consumers has become aware of what companies are up to and are rewarding the ones doing good things.

The reason I loved Oprah's *Big Give* is because she promoted the idea of creative benevolence. And yes, the network and sponsors made money. Yes, people were entertained. Yes, lives were changed for the better. Yes, yes, yes. Oprah gave us a great example of doing well by doing good. She could have chosen to fire people who were not cold-blooded business people, but she chose to be innovative. I believe that at its heart, this way of doing business is an "innovation" challenge. We need to think differently about the situation and not make it a moral one.

That is the thought my business partner, Raff Vitón, came back with after attending a Conscious Capitalism conference recently. (Go to http://www.consciouscapitalism.org/)

"To whom much is given, much is required."

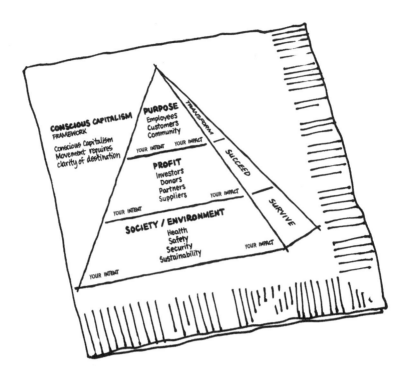

Conscious Capitalism is a new way of thinking about your business model: higher quality inputs = higher net income. It's NOT a new way of thinking about "social responsibility"—instead, it's the idea that an organization has an obligation to act in not only its own best interests but to create value for all of its stakeholders (e.g., customers, employees, suppliers, investors, society) as well.

On the way back from the conference, Raff sketched the conscious capitalism framework in a way that borrows from Abraham Maslow and his well-known hierarchy of needs, because he thought it paralleled what good business looks like.

The line on the right side of the chart shows that any conscious capitalism movement requires clarity of destination. In our case we want Maddock Douglas to be known as a company that makes money—the middle layer—but more important, we want our people to know what we believe (our purpose) so that everyone here can work effectively in unison (which in turn will allow us to make more money for our stakeholders and make more contributions to society).

Because of that, we don't cast the issue of social responsibility in terms of "earthmuffins" versus "plunderers." Not only is that dichotomy not helpful, it is not particularly accurate. It is better to talk about "going green" the way Ray Anderson of Interface, Inc. or Jeff Imelt of GE do: "It is a way of making more money."

It is also why it is much easier to sell a plan to reduce accidents by saying, "If we create a safer work environment, we will save money on insurance and manpower costs," than it is to run around screaming about the exploitation of the workforce.

I don't know who said it at the conference, but they got the idea absolutely right: "Conscious capitalism is a devastatingly good weapon." It is not an end in itself, but a tool.

Creating a win-win-win business model—with the wins being the ones that benefit the company, its stakeholders and the environment/society in general—is the only way to optimize value. Since that is true, that means, in addition to measuring your success monetarily, you also need to create new additional metrics that will tangibly illustrate the ongoing progress toward the interrelated desired outcomes. At the onset, it could be as simple as charting your recycling efforts or as complex as measuring the ROI on your employee safety efforts.

As an Idea Monkey and entrepreneur, I strongly believe it will be capitalism, not either government or charity, that creates the kind of world we want our kids and grandkids to grow up in. Getting that world will require innovative thinking ... but it is well worth the trip for many reasons, including a customer base that rewards you for doing the right things. But, again, if you just see this as a way to make more money—and it is—you are missing part of the point.

Build a business:
- **with a "purpose" (and to make money)**
- **that creates value for stakeholders**
- **that's led by a conscious Leader (continually focused on personal development – a "learner")**
- **that contributes to a more conscious culture**

As a friend once put it, we may not ultimately save the world, but it's important that our kids know we were on the right team and we were trying.

I am proud to say that our company is a huge believer in the idea of doing well by doing good. We are proud of the clients we represent and the contributions—both financial and in-kind—that we make. We believe in giving to charities, supporting talented kids with scholarships, letting our creative folks use their brains to support benevolent projects, and using our resources, financial and other, to do the right thing. To us, not only is that good business, it is totally  consistent with the kind of company we want to run—it aligns with our purpose and our core values.

And yes, we totally ripped off Oprah's *Big Give* as a way to celebrate Christmas a couple of years ago. There were four teams who changed the lives of four families. Guess what? Everybody won.

SAVING THE WORLD—THROUGH INNOVATION

President Obama is still in office as I write this, and with the economic crisis, the health care crisis and the BP oil disaster, the history he is helping create will certainly be fascinating to review. But it is a bit unfair to talk about his policies since we don't know how they will ultimately play out, so for now, let's turn our attention to his predecessor.

During his second term, President Bush announced a plan to stop the growth of greenhouse gases in the U.S. by 2025, acknowledging the need to head off serious climate change.

Regardless of your political views, it was clear this was a major public policy initiative—one that reminded us of another announced a half century ago. In 1961, President Kennedy declared: "I believe that this nation should commit itself to achieving the goal, before this decade is out, of landing a man on the moon and returning him safely to the earth. No single space project ... will be more exciting, or more impressive to mankind, or more important ... and none will be so difficult or expensive to accomplish. ... "

Show of hands: who really thought President Bush's announcement will lead to innovative change?

Sadly, just as there was under Presidents Clinton, George H. Bush, Reagan and Carter, there has been a lot of talk about a radically new environmental policy, but very little action. (In fact, the inconvenient truth here is that Bush's policy actually allows for a continued growth of carbon emissions until the 2025 deadline.)

Think of a major initiative in your company. Who is the <u>one</u> person in charge?

Still, there are great lessons for leaders here. Why was Kennedy successful at mobilizing the country while subsequent presidents have not been? And to broaden the question, how do the most innovative organizations (and their leaders) move past the rhetoric and actually produce results?

From our experience, effective innovation leadership involves three elements: a bold declaration, accountability and tracking key metrics. Let's take them one at a time.

Declare It. People love to be led, to envision, to aspire and to dream. We naturally gravitate toward a cause. Revolutionary companies chase big dreams. Microsoft pictured a computer on every desk; Walmart envisioned affordability for the masses. Each started with a bold declaration. Each declaration came from a person (Bill Gates, Sam Walton) who was committed to following through and keeping the leadership around him accountable.

Account for It. (Ring)leaders know that accountability is key. It was reported that President Bush met every day following September 11, 2001, with his national security adviser to review the top 20 on the most-wanted terrorist list. He was committed to fighting terrorism. As president, he was clearly accountable. To date there has been no further terrorist attack in the United States.

A committed (Ring)leader implicitly asks the same question in every meeting: "How does this help us get to our vision?" That's what happens after you make a sincere declaration—if you are serious.

When it comes to accountability, the question to ask is this: Who is the one person in charge of turning the big idea into reality? Our experience is that if you don't have a single individual who is accountable, your declaration is in trouble. Read: it will likely fail. If one person is not accountable, then nobody is accountable.

Your chief innovation officer, or whoever is accountable, must institutionalize the processes, and the behaviors that lead to a culture of rigor, risk and results. Innovation can give you an amazing competitive advantage. But without accountability, it becomes an expensive and demoralizing exercise.

Track It. Finally, if you want to see progress, you need to employ Peter Drucker's famous phrase: "What gets measured gets done."

So if you are serious, here are some items to measure and evaluate:

People/Policies/Culture

- How many people are dedicated to the initiative?
- How much training is being done?
- Does leadership sponsor key initiatives?
- Are incentives aligned to drive key initiatives?

Process/Resources

- Is there a formal process in your organization?
- Does your process track—and allow for—failures as well as successes?
- How much time does an initiative take from idea to profit?
- What does your innovation portfolio look like?

Results

- How much does each initiative drive ROI (return on innovation) portfolio management (revenue, margin, time in market)?
- Which metrics will keep you focused and make your declaration a reality?

THE FRUIT OF YOUR DECLARATION

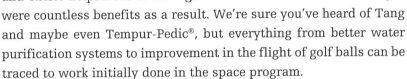

President Kennedy made a declaration and NASA helped see it through. And there were countless benefits as a result. We're sure you've heard of Tang and maybe even Tempur-Pedic®, but everything from better water purification systems to improvement in the flight of golf balls can be traced to work initially done in the space program.

And admire them or not (I choose to admire them), both Bill Gates and Sam Walton made the lives of hundreds of millions of people better. For your country, and your company, you need to create an innovation program that is both daring and tracked closely, otherwise you will just join the long list of people—many presidents among them—who made sweeping announcements that were doomed to be forgotten because nothing was done to ensure they happened.

Mr. President, may we suggest a "Director of Homeland Innovation?" Please?

DO IT! (NOW!)

There has never been a better time to innovate. However, it takes an entrepreneurial mind-set.

Consider:

- Matt Kuttler, known for building a promotional products business, is now reinventing the way small business supplies are purchased at ReStockIt.com.
- Rick Jamieson, known for building accounting businesses, is now bent on creating the greenest brake pad company at ABS Friction.

- Marty Renkis, known for building an online training company, is now bent on reinventing digital, wireless security systems at SmartVue.com.

And proving that you don't even have to go far afield to find new opportunities:

- Brad Handelman, known for being the largest manufacturer of bowling bags, is now putting any high resolution image you want on bowling pins and balls at: Ontheballbowling.com.

These are not just dreams. They are ideas that were quickly turned into multimillion-dollar businesses by people who saw a need, had an idea about how to fill it, and experimented until they got the formula right.

Entrepreneurs like these should be your role models because no matter what is happening in the economy, they constantly ask "what if?" They are constantly examining—and re-examining—opportunities most of the people in your company will overlook. They are early adopters. They are innovators. They fail quickly and fail often, but they fail forward. They are risk takers.

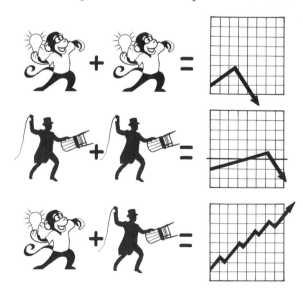

(RING)LEADER To-Dos

Recast issues in terms of "and" thinking as in "you can do X, which will increase earnings *and* it will contribute to the greater good."

Choose to be a conscious leader; build a conscious business with higher purpose that transcends profit maximization.

Create win-win-wins for all stakeholders – in the long run, higher quality inputs = higher net incomes.

DO **GOOD** THINGS.

Bring joy to other people's lives.

And make more $$.

NAME FIVE PEOPLE WHO BRING OUT THE BEST IN YOU
AND WHY. (WHAT ARE YOU GOING TO DO TO MAKE THEM
A MORE IMPORTANT PART OF YOUR LIFE?)

> _____
_____
_____

> _____
_____
_____

> _____
_____
_____

> _____
_____
_____

> _____
_____
_____

Chapter 12

Discovering a Yin to Your Yang

Or Are You a Walt Disney or a Roy Disney?

Perhaps no other country celebrates innovation the way America does.

This passion for inventions started early in our history. Did you know that George Washington signed the first U.S. Patent Grant on July 31, 1790, and the patent examiner was none other than

Thomas Jefferson? (Thank you, Google. [Google, by the way, is patent

To see what makes Google Google, go to
http://www.google.com/patents?vid=6285999

number 6285999 filed January 9, 1998; issued September 4, 2001.])

In America, we're reminded of the life-changing power of inventiveness every day. Some of the greatest inventors of yesterday spawned the greatest brands of today. What do the names Chrysler, Coleman, Goodyear, Campbell, Colt and Edison mean to you? Cars, tents, tires, soup, guns and the electric light bulb, of course.

But when you dig a little deeper, you start to notice an incredibly important aspect of inventiveness: for every yin, there is a yang. For example, the next time you are marveling at the wonders of Disney, make sure you remember Roy. While Walt was dreaming about his Magic Kingdom and making a mouse talk, his brother Roy was actually making sure that Walt's dreams would come true. Roy was the operational genius; a yin for Walt's yang.

> **Are you a Walt or a Roy?**
> Either answer is great as long as you know what makes you feel strong.

For every Idea Monkey who says coming up with new concepts is a piece of cake, there are others who say executing is easy. These are the operational experts—the Roy Disneys if you will—who know how to drive the best ideas forward. The corporate equivalent of Roy would be the COOs. You don't think of them as product innovators, but once they have an idea, or are presented with one, they execute it.

IT'S TRUE FOR ME, TOO

In 2008, *BusinessWeek* published a photograph of Raphael (Raff) Louis Vitón, the president of Maddock Douglas, and me to complement our column "The Innovation Engine." (Both the column and the picture are still running.)

The picture was a photo-retouched beauty constructed by one of their artists who arranged two separate head shots into what most describe as "a lovely engagement picture."

Soon after, everyone in our office was calling us "Siegfried and Roy, The Ambiguously Innovative Duo"—not (to pay tribute to Seinfeld) that there's anything wrong with that.

As the old saying goes, behind every joke there is some truth. The folks at Maddock Douglas know the truth. Raff and I are a dynamic duo. For me, ideas are easy—but execution? Not so much. For Raff, the exact opposite is true.

And that is invariably the case. That is something that I learned from the first days we opened our doors.

For example, Hank Adams walked confidently into our office in the spring of 1995. He and his classmate and business partner, Eric Carbone, had an idea. They wanted to use the extremely new Internet technology to create "the world's first online sports bar." They imagined an online destination where people could talk smack with their friends who went to a rival college, buy pro and college merchandise, and maybe even wager on a game. Hank had played college football and, as a graduate student at Northwestern, he saw an opportunity to keep sports central to his life.

Not only was the Internet new, but the whole idea of a virtual meeting place was no less than revolutionary.

For the next six months, we helped Hank and Eric build their vision. Research, prototypes and meetings were held in which we helped them think through both creative and operational challenges.

Their partnership was a classic example of Monkey and (Ring)leader. Hank had a million ideas and Eric was charged with seeing the best ideas through (and keeping costs under control, since money was tight).

In the end, Extreme Fans® was born. As it turns out, their vision was spot on. Extreme Fans was purchased by AOL and eventually became their channel for sports. Today, nearly 30 million fantasy football players would agree that Hank and Eric were on to something in 1995. Both Hank and Eric will tell you that they could not have created Extreme Fans without each other.

> You either feel strongest brainstorming ideas or you feel strongest getting them to market. Pick one and find a partner who is good at the other.
>
> My experience: you can be average at both or you can find a partner and be brilliant at one of them.

By the way, Hank didn't give up on sports innovation. He's now the CEO of Sportvision and you see his work every weekend. You know that yellow first-down line that magically appears during football broadcasts? Hank is responsible for this and other innovations. In 2010, Sportvision was named as one of the top 100 most innovative companies by *Fast Company Magazine*.

When I told Hank I thought he was an Idea Monkey, here's what he said: "Monkey? Yeah, I guess I get a lot of juice from seeing ideas come to life. When I look back, much of my energy comes from having the idea and then handing the ball off to a partner who keeps things moving. I've learned—sometimes the hard way—that every brain-stormer is only as good as the operators he surrounds himself with."

Hank was lucky to have Eric and Eric was lucky to have Hank. Walt was lucky to have Roy and Roy was lucky to have Walt. Who is the Yin for your Yang?

COMPANIES, TOO, ARE EITHER YINS OR YANGS

Turns out, the best companies are a lot like Roy and Walt Disney. Everything we said about people applies to companies as well. Some are better at having ideas; others are better at making the idea happen.

All too often, we here at Maddock Douglas (and maybe at your firm, too) stop at the first part and pat ourselves on the back for being innovative, even though we aren't exactly sure what to do with a great idea.

At our firm, ideas come easily. In fact, we believe big, beautiful, million-dollar ideas are a dime a dozen. Want to see? Picture yourself sitting on a plane. Hmmm. Let's see. Airline ideas. Why don't airlines create a loyalty card? You'd pay for travel at the beginning of the year in exchange for some sort of special treatment or perks—say, no fees for checking luggage, free food and drinks (including alcohol), and access to their "president's club" lounges so you would have someplace—other than the gate—to wait for your plane. Sure, you can pay à la carte for all these things, but it would be more convenient for you if the airline bundled it all together, and better for the airlines since they would get the money up front. Starbucks has created plenty of cash flow with this idea. Why not the airlines?

Here's another idea: airlines should sell luggage engineered to fit perfectly into their planes. The airlines get new revenue and quicker boarding because bags are all fitting nicely into place. You get the picture.

Once again, for all of us who say ideas are easy, there are others who say executing is easy. Give these people a big idea, and they execute flawlessly. Think about clothing retailers like The Limited or the Gap. They spot a hot fashion item (the idea) and figure out a way to make it appeal to everyone who does not fly to Paris for the latest runway show.

As we said, we find that companies, like people, are usually good at either creating ideas or executing them. The trick is to know which describes your company. If you or your organization are about operational excellence but desperate for big ideas, consider importing this kind of thinking via a business partner.

Want proof that we are on the right track about this idea? Consider venture capitalists. VC companies are full of Roy Disneys and they know it, so they don't waste time trying to think up new ideas. They know what they are good at—execution. They find people with the big, new idea and help them bring it to market.

EQUAL, BUT NOT SEPARATE

Perhaps one of the clearest example of Yin and Yangs are songwriting duos: Richard Rodgers (music) and Oscar Hammerstein II (lyrics); Elton John (music) and Bernie Taupin (lyrics) ... Bon Jovi and Sambora ... Axl Rose and Slash ... OK, I'll stop.

If you could still talk to these duos, they would be quick to tell you that there is NOT an absolute delineation of duties all the time. The lyricists will suggest a mood/tempo ("maybe we should do it as a jazz waltz") and the person creating the tune will suggest a phrase or maybe even the title.

There isn't resentment when this happens. They are trying to create the best song possible.

That should be your approach when you are coming up with new ideas. Even though the roles of Yin and Yang are clearly defined, ideas should be welcome from anywhere.

IDEAS
WELCOME
FROM
ANYWHERE

(RING)LEADER To-Dos

Be deliberate about your staffing – if you have "Walt's," find "Roy's" – and vice versa. Be careful though; if they are not self-aware enough to truly value what the other brings to the table, they will be dangerous.

Strive for balance. Too many Monkeys = tons of ideas and poor execution. Too many (Ring)leaders = masterful execution with too little innovation.

Fire Monkeys who don't appreciate (Ring)leaders.

Fire (Ring)leaders who don't value Monkeys.

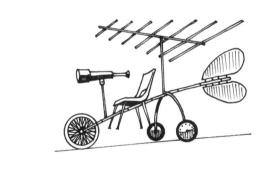

(You must be ready to doodle by now!)

Chapter 13
The David Strategies

When it comes to innovation, David almost always beats Goliath. I know if you work for a large company, you don't want to hear it, but it is true.

That's why while the rest of us are dreaming of missing the final exam for a course we never took, you, an executive of a large company, keep having nightmares about the maverick firm that is about to put you out of business with an industry-changing product or service that makes your beloved Goliath Inc. obsolete.

History shows you have the right to be worried. Whoever thought that GM would ever find itself struggling for its very existence while Japanese car companies thrive, or a once tiny regional institution known as North Carolina National Bank would end up owning Merrill Lynch?

To allow you to sleep easier at night, let's examine three strategies that small and midsize companies constantly employ against you, and talk about what you can do to counter. (If you work for a small firm, double check that you are employing all three approaches.)

DAVID STRATEGY #1: BEING JUST RIGHT ENOUGH

There is an old axiom about business leaders needing to be right only 51 percent of the time. The practice of constant experimentation is as fundamental to research as it is to innovation: try, fail, learn; try, fail, learn; try, succeed, repeat (see Chapter 6).

When you are small, you benefit from a quick cycle of experimentation and learning. When you are big, the budgets, culture and shareholders all stand in your way. If you are a Goliath, you may look at your innovation team and notice that nothing revolutionary is hitting the market. If that is the case, chances are they are afraid of failing. After all, if nothing launches, nothing can fail, and therefore they can't be blamed. (So from a personal survival point of view, within a corporation it is better to kill an idea than to launch it.)

As a (Ring)leader, you must demand small, controlled launches that allow your teams to learn, build courage and taste success. Imagine what would happen if you told your team that it was okay to break even, or (gasp) lose money in the short term, if they were reasonably sure they would learn enough from the failure to increase the chances of succeeding next time around? Rather than imagining it, look down the street. That's the strategy David & Co. are employing.

DAVID STRATEGY #2: ATTACK TRADITION

Show me a mature business, and I will show you either a superannuated management team that wants to freeze time or an entrenched union keeping the company from doing what is necessary.

If you are in a mature industry, you are surrounded by inertia, habit, tradition, complacency and "expertise"—people who know the best way something should be done (i.e., it's the way it has always been done). You've been in the room with these people. They can give you 10 reasons why any new idea won't work, "based on my experience."

All this produces amazing opportunities for upstart companies to beat you with innovation. You need to look no further than the

music industry (see iTunes), the travel industry (see Orbitz), the video industry (see Netflix®). I could go on, but you get the idea.

How do you eliminate this problem? The obvious answer is to slash bureaucracy; fire the people who are hindering progress and beef up your innovation efforts. The less obvious course? Think like an entrepreneur and create a new company of your own.

We see this all the time. Bright, shiny people in large companies filled with piss, vinegar and ideas. They are passionate. They are idealistic and oftentimes they are spot on.

If this is you, and you feel like you are losing your edge, we'd coach you to view your job as research. Think: when I start my own firm or manage a team, how would I do things differently?

If you manage a person like this, we'd coach you to start a skunk-works project or empower this person in some way. If you don't, you risk losing them emotionally first and physically second.

DAVID STRATEGY #3: THE APPROVAL OF THE KING

Nothing maintains momentum like C-level support. Unlike giant companies, midsize and small companies benefit from the involvement of the CEO. When the CEO sponsors an idea, you can bet it is approved (in record time). Remember the cycle: try, fail, learn? CEO support allows you to run this cycle quickly and often.

"We want the CEO on our team."

Most Goliath CEOs talk about innovation, but they simply can't be involved with the day-to-day innovation initiatives. If you are the CEO, you need to be involved. If you aren't the Ultimate Idea Monkey, you need to garner as much upper-level management support for your new idea as possible. If you don't, the odds of nothing happening increase dramatically.

A final thought about strategies 1, 2 and 3: in the Old Testament, David picks up a stone and with his slingshot, hurls it at Goliath, toppling an opponent thought to be invincible. There has never been a better metaphor for innovation.

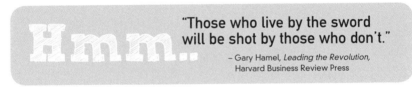

Hmm...

"Those who live by the sword will be shot by those who don't."

– Gary Hamel, *Leading the Revolution*, Harvard Business Review Press

HOW TO BE LIKE DAVID

I've talked about three strategies you could employ to be more entrepreneurial. Here, let's provide three tactics as well.

1. **Take a lot of small bites.** Big businesses must try to create big wins because their costs for launching new products are so high. It is not uncommon for our clients to ask for a $100 million return from a single launch. Entrepreneurs can hardly fathom the type of budgets that typically support one of these "mega-projects," yet they often manage to bootstrap their way to the kind of results these big firms are seeking.

How? Two words: small bites. Small bites means:

- Trying 10 ideas in the time it takes large companies to roll out one.
- Using the Internet to test four different media and creative strategies instead of rolling out an expensive print campaign.
- Trying four different business models simultaneously to see which one has legs.
- Working with multiple partners to test launch an idea to learn about the idea and the partnership at the same time.
- Doing all of this with a "fast and cheap" attitude.

> "Entrepreneur: The type of personality who is willing to take upon herself or himself a new venture or enterprise and accepts full responsibility for the outcome."
>
> *−Wikipedia*

Here is a trend worth noting. It used to be that innovation consultancies were hired to help with ideation, research and process. The underlying theme I see today is these firms are being asked to help large companies move more quickly. Said differently, leaders are focused on getting their teams out of their own way. They want them to act more entrepreneurial.

2. Hit them when they least expect it. When was the last time you thought about taking on a giant? Grainger, the leading global broad-line supplier of facilities maintenance products, does about $7 billion annually in sales. A few years back, The Home Depot gave Grainger a scare when it spent $3.5 billion to buy Hughes Supply, a direct competitor. By making the move, The Home Depot was declaring war. As one might have expected, Grainger reacted aggressively with public relations and marketing. The counter-attack, coupled with the housing market downturn, seemed to put The Home Depot on its heels. With the threat gone, Grainger went back to business as usual.

That was entrepreneur Matt Kuttler's cue. He started ReStockit.com, which offers a total of 200,000 restaurant supplies, office supplies, electronics and tools.

"The fact is, it's usually way easier to compete with large companies than small ones," says Kuttler. "They are set in their ways—we're not. We can test ideas more quickly to better serve the customer. Most businesses are afraid to wake the sleeping giant. That's where we find the most opportunity." Not surprisingly, Kuttler's company continues to grow far faster than either Grainger or The Home Depot.

3. Use the Alpha SWOT Analysis. Typically SWOT—or strengths, weaknesses, opportunities and threats—analysis is used to identify internal opportunities. Now may be the time to turn a modified version—let's call it the Alpha Small Business SWOT—on your competitors.

Here's how. You use the same four letters, asking a question about each.

- S = **Sneakiness.** How can we do something our most beaten-down competitors would never be prepared for?
- W = **Will.** What would break their spirit right now? What would make them lose faith in their strategy?
- O = **Offense.** What are the top 10 aggressive tactics we can employ immediately that would hurt our competitors the most?
- T = **Thinking (radically).** How can we redefine the marketplace, leaving the competition scrambling to catch up?

By using any one of these three techniques, you can assemble an aggressive, simple (David-like) strategy.

Go get 'em!

CONSIDER SCRAPPING THE BUSINESS PLAN

Adaptability is the hallmark of a great entrepreneur, no matter what you may have been taught in school.

Find an honest entrepreneur and she will tell you she has changed directions so many times that her business has little in common with the initial business plan.

The point isn't that business plans—or the annual plan you prepare for your company—are worthless. On the contrary. They are an excellent way to envision, create strategy, raise funds and test ideas. But sometimes sticking with the plan is the worst thing to do.

Entrepreneurs know that freezing up, running away or laying low just aren't options that will work for them. They would rather fail spectacularly than sit still and have the market do it to them.

For Maddock Douglas, 2001 marked a dramatic turning point in our business. In hindsight, I am certain the horrific events on September 11 pushed everyone—including our management team—to reconsider what really mattered. This was helped along by the fact that business just plain stopped as people tried to get a handle on what had just happened. During this crazy time, rethinking our position in the market seemed to be a natural thing to do. So after a decade of growth, we rebooted our business and began to focus more on innovation. Failure was absolutely a possibility, but the market was telling us the old business model was dying.

Scrapping our existing plan worked. Our business has more than quadrupled in size since then.

If you have a solid strategy, double down when the going gets tough. If you don't have a solid strategy, use market pressure as an opportunity to rethink where you're heading.

THE ALPHA EFFECT

If you want to attract and retain your most creative and ingenious Idea Monkeys (some companies refer to them as their "Alphas"), you must feed their hunger to innovate.

As I touched on earlier, much of what I've read and certainly everything I have experienced running our firm tells me that the keys to attracting and retaining the best employees—the Alphas—are making sure they are working on something:

A. meaningful,

B. in a lower stress environment, and

C. with a reward system that makes sense.

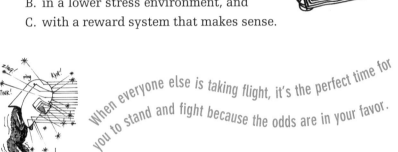

When everyone else is taking flight, it's the perfect time for you to stand and fight because the odds are in your favor.

Now think about the person in your company who everyone looks up to. What do you most appreciate about her? I bet you name such characteristics as action-oriented, driven, passionate, fun and genuine.

Importantly, these three criteria for Alpha attraction and retention are quite obviously linked through innovation.

Alphas naturally move into roles with greater challenges and opportunities to learn and make a difference. It isn't about money. Money follows these types of people because they follow the challenges. They find them and master both problems and opportunities and get well paid for doing so.

So being innovation focused naturally attracts Alphas, and this in turn drives a better culture. Here's why: successful innovation is intrinsically meaningful. Said differently, you have to be solving a significant need in order to have success with a new product or service. The best and happiest employees want to work on something meaningful. So they naturally gravitate toward innovation assignments. It is not only more fun but also has a greater potential for personal payoff. The sustainability innovation megatrend makes this point even more valid.

Innovation is typically on the radar of the CEO. If you want to be in the spotlight, take on a major innovation initiative. It will bring out the best in you as an employee and get you immediately recognized and rewarded for performance. Ironically, we've seen people aggressively rewarded whether their particular project was a market success or not. It was the act of "taking on the important stuff" that got them extra credit from on high.

IDEA MONKEYS ARE NATURALLY ENTREPRENEURIAL

So it is no surprise that when you piss off a Monkey, they are just as likely to use their ideas to start their own business as they are to help yours.

Back to that Alpha who left your team. In hindsight, what would you have done to keep her happy? Chances are you would eagerly put her on your most heady, rewarding challenges. Think about what would happen if you had a project like that for every Alpha in the organization. The result would be a magnetic culture that attracts and retains the best people. It would be the Alpha Effect. Instead, too often we ask our best people to handle our most difficult clients, or profitable, but uninspiring projects. That leads to an unfortunate exodus of talented people.

Change the way you treat your Alphas and you will hang on to more of them. I guarantee it.

DEFENDING THE VENTURE CAPITALISTS

Nearly every entrepreneur who took venture capital money during the past 40 years will tell you pretty much the same story: the VCs exerted far more control than expected, budgets were slashed, friends were fired from the payroll, and "they never really got our vision." Given those stories, you'd think that venture capitalists are the last thing the world needs to make innovation happen. However, they may be exactly what's needed.

> "What was working for the company that bought my company like? It was like some other guy was sleeping with my wife—I had to watch and he wasn't that good."
>
> —wishes to remain anonymous

(go figure)

Sure, it used to be that VCs were about cutting costs and relentlessly narrowing the company's vision to create a firm that was easy to sell or take public. But today, the smartest VCs are changing their focus. They are looking for three things:

Disrupters, aka companies that are reinventing the rules: Companies that can produce a result through a product or a service that is dramatically more effective or cheaper than what their peers are doing. We aren't talking about incremental improvements here. We are talking about firms like PayPal, who earlier in this decade helped change the way we buy things. Or Lending Tree, which took the control away from banks when it came to making mortgage loans.

Pay-for-performance cultures: These are companies that believe in linking pay to key metrics and sharing the data with everyone so they know exactly where they stand and what it takes to get ahead. This open-book mentality was unheard of two decades ago. But today it is empowering growing companies to build cultures of accountability—an extreme competitive advantage.

If you spend time with today's fast-growth companies, it becomes immediately apparent that the trend toward open-book management is real and powerful. VCs love this trend. They are happy to pay for performance—it is the basis of their business model. So if I were a VC for a day, I'd be looking for companies that keep their books open. I'd never have to worry about my money, because everyone in the company would be watching it as if it were their own. Jack Stack wrote a great playbook for this concept based on his own experience. Check out *The Great Game of Business.*

Failing forward: To be an innovator, you must be prepared to fail often. Companies that have demonstrated the tenacity and skill it takes to make small bets on many failures and then invest on the idea that works are where we would put our money. They are, in fact, acting like a VC. Today, as soon as your idea hits the market, someone will be copying it. So a company must be constantly innovating to stay ahead of the curve. VCs are beginning to recognize that this pattern of—try, fail, learn; try, fail, learn; try, succeed, repeat—is a critical cultural attribute for successful, fast-growth companies.

It's easy to dismiss VCs as greedy S.O.Bs. But their interest and yours are in perfect alignment. They want to create companies that succeed.

NAME THE THREE BIGGEST PLAYERS IN YOUR INDUSTRY AND WHAT YOU CAN DO THAT THEY CANNOT OR WOULD NOT DO.

> _____

_____

_____

> _____

_____

_____

> _____

_____

_____

(RING)LEADER To-Dos

Try, fail, learn; try fail learn; try, succeed, repeat.

Interrogate reality – attack traditions and unexamined assumptions.

Take small bites – think simultaneous experiments (fast and cheap) before you go big.

Hit them where they ain't looking ... and the odds are, they ain't.

Be aggressive.

WRITE THREE THINGS YOU WOULD DO IN LIFE OR BUSINESS IF YOU HAD UNLIMITED BUDGET:

> _____

_____

_____

> _____

_____

_____

> _____

_____

_____

(Now think: Is it really the money that is stopping you? Really?!)

Chapter 14
Solving the Innovation Nightmare:
Why You Need To Be Ruthless

"iiiiinnnnnhnnnnnnooooooooooovvaaaatttiiiooon!!!"

Question:
If a CEO yells "innovation" in the forest but his management
team covers their ears, did he really yell anything at all?

The news cameras roll as the CEO of one of the nation's largest companies boldly outlines his well thought-out, incredibly detailed vision for changing his dinosaur industry. "Innovation will be the cornerstone from which we build our future," he says. "For too long, we have relied on our great brand, loyal customers and fine work-force to carry the day. But the world is changing and our customers and shareholders are counting on us to deliver new products and new services. Our competitors haven't recognized this fact. But we have. So from this day forward, I commit to create a culture of innovation. We will be known as the company that reinvented our industry."

The next day, a huge plaque is hung in the corporate lobby that boldly proclaims "Core Value #1: Innovation." And you can tell that the CEO believes this with all his heart. Like Paul on the road to Damascus, he has seen the light.

In the aftermath of the announcement, we at Maddock Douglas applaud. (Innovation is our business after all.) Wall Street applauds—and the stock price rises. And there is a renewed optimism among the rank and file in the halls of the sleepy company.

And then something unfortunate happens. Nothing.

Nothing happens.

Nothing at all.

After a blizzard of memos outlining what the "new" company is going to look like, nothing changes. Why? Blame it on the inevitable outcome when a bull meets a grizzly bear—and a bunch of his friends—in the woods.

THE REAL BEARS IN THE WOODS

In the world of investments, there are bears and there are bulls. The bears say things are going to get worse and the bulls optimistically and aggressively place bets that not only won't that be the case, but that everything is going to get better.

In the world of corporate innovation, the bullish CEO ("We can reinvent our industry") is often a bull who makes the unfortunate mistake of surrounding himself with bears.

I love bullish CEOs, but I am pretty sick of working with bears. Bears tend to nod a lot in meetings and then passive aggressively do everything in their power to keep any significant change from happening. To the CEO's face they say innovation effort is, in fact, truly needed. When he is out of sight, they whisper to everyone in the senior ranks that things are just fine as they are. (All of us here on the executive level have jobs, don't we?)

ATTACK OF THE BUZZ KILLERS

MOTIVATION

It is incredible how many companies are run by bulls who surround themselves with bears—and surround is the right word. The pure-of-heart CEO is hopelessly outnumbered. And so nothing happens.

For fans of innovation, this is like a football team owner who promises the Super Bowl, but spends no money on free agency. Eventually the fans—the stockholders, the partners, the employees—give up. They stop believing. They find another team.

You're not a CEO? That's not the point. If you are a leader, you are a de facto CEO. Someone is counting on you to make them believe or get them focused on something that they can fully embrace. You need to get ruthless and address the elephant, uh, I mean bear, in the room.

BE RUTHLESS

When I am speaking in front of a large group, I like to ask leaders if they believe that they are ultimately going to be successful at their current endeavor. Not surprisingly, the majority say "yes." Then I ask them if they think everyone on their team thinks that they will be successful. And, *quite* surprisingly, the majority of the leaders say "no."

Then comes the hard part. I ask them why they don't go back to the office and fire all the nonbelievers. Don't these people work for you? Don't you think that they are going to deliver the exact outcome that they expect? Don't you think good leadership starts with making everyone believe in the vision or getting the nonbelievers off the bus?

Blank stares.

Hey (Ring)leader, you deserve the staff you get.

Much has been written about leaders who had a vision or a dream and, through blood, sweat and tears, made their dream a reality. Successful entrepreneurs like Ford, Jobs and Dell moved beyond declaring and got busy doing. In the course of their journey, lots and lots of people were fired because they did not or could not believe. It may have manifested itself as poor work performance, but at the heart of the matter they just didn't believe enough in the vision to make it happen.

I once had a business friend tell me he had completely transformed the culture of his company. He said that they now had one of the most happy, engaged and productive organizations he had ever run. When I asked him how he had created such a culture, his response was simple: "I fired all the unhappy people."

In the book *What Happy People Know*, author Dan Baker describes an optimist as "a person who believes something positive is going to come from even the most brutal experience." I love this definition. Unfortunately, it puts a spotlight on how so many Monkeys fail: they look at a bearish teammate as a potential positive outcome rather than what he is: a liability.

This book has utilized a whole bunch of ink to get across how critical optimism, gratefulness and sense of wonder are to the Idea Monkey and to the inventive organization. But the most inventive people and organizations understand something else, something that you must as well. They are ruthless when it comes to nonbelievers. They don't put up with them, and if you want to be successful, you can't either.

WHAT IS TO BE DONE?

I know this chapter may come across as a bit cynical, but I am a truly hopeless optimist, so let's get to some solutions.

> " If you believe you can or believe you can't, you're right."
> Henry Ford

If you are a bullish Idea Monkey or (Ring)leader, here are a few tips that will absolutely make your corporate lives better—and more fulfilling.

Let's start with counsel for the CEOs or head Monkey—whether you have the title or not.

HIRE BELIEVERS

If you have people on your staff who don't really believe change is possible or that the old way is good enough, for God's sake, release them to find a more fulfilling destiny. If you don't have the guts to do it, then please stop saying that you are going to change the world because your people simply won't let it happen and you are going to look like a fool.

HIRE OBJECTIVE SENIOR MANAGERS

This is a nice way of saying that you should bring in leaders from outside your industry. Einstein said, "One should not expect to solve a problem with the same level of intelligence that caused it." Einstein was really smart (about management, too, as it turns out). If you have people leading your research, marketing and strategy group with a combined 40 years of industry experience, they are about to help

> "GET OUT AND DON'T COME BACK UNTIL YOU HAVE MUCH LESS INDUSTRY EXPERIENCE!"

you break your promise to your shareholders. Said differently, they are rolling their eyes at you. "You don't get it," they are saying behind your back. They know the rules. They know what's possible. They know what can and can't be done. They can and will bend the data to prove their points. Meanwhile, a competitive team with a combined zero years of industry experience is about to reinvent your industry.

They are going to deliver on the promise you made to Wall Street. You must go find those really smart, really capable, really courageous risk takers and offer them jobs. They will get it done. They will help you keep your promise. They believe. Most of your current team does not.

PROMOTE FAILURE

Entrepreneurs understand that each small failure brings them closer to the solution. So find ways to demand lots of baby-step failures that promote learning and create a culture of action. This will get you to the finish line and keep fear of failure from locking up your innovation engine.

Now on to the innovation leaders who report directly to the CEO:

LISTEN TO THE YOUNGSTERS

They can see things that you cannot. Remember when you used to be the youngest person in the room and all the terrific ideas you had (but had problems getting implemented)?

FAIL FORWARD

Get into the habit of creating many experiments and celebrating the learning, no matter the outcome, e.g., "in this experiment, we learned that people did not understand our offer; in this experiment we learned we were charging too much; in this experiment we learned that the button had to be in a different place." Each "failure" is actually a success because the team has learned something important and has moved one step closer toward getting it right.

CONTROL THE FRAMING

Every company has its own language when it comes to the innovation process. As we mentioned earlier, many times this language has been linked to past projects. For example, the last team that created a "working prototype" may have overinvested in the experience and created unrealistic expectations for your team. That's why we encourage you to invent your own innovation language. For example, calling something a "feedback concept" may be better than calling it a working prototype. If you control the language, you control the expectations.

Finally ...

QUIT

If you find yourself so afraid, so burnt-out, so cynical that you can't believe that a big idea is about to happen, it is time to move on to the next challenge. You have the smarts, the experience, the skills to become an amazing change agent *in another industry*! Go find it. Your new peers will be amazed at how you can see things that they can't and have the solutions that have eluded them.

WHY INNOVATION IS REALLY BEGINNER'S LUCK

What if your boss has been an industry expert for decades? What if he keeps talking about innovation? What if your gut tells you he is about to fail again? Bad news, your gut is right.

Matt Kuttler founded, built and sold a promotions products company, PhoneCard Express. Now he is running an office supply company, ReStockIt.com, another firm of his own invention. Rick Jamieson built and sold a successful accounting company. Now he is busy reinventing the automobile service industry as CEO of ABS Friction. Mike Michalowicz started a successful technology integration firm, then built and sold a data forensics company.

At first glance, it may appear as if these guys are really lucky. They may even tell you so. Dig deeper and you'll see they have the very thing you don't look for when you hire your leaders: inexperience.

Each and every time, they started a firm in an industry that they knew almost nothing about. And therein lies a lesson for you.

You like to hire people who know everything about the way business is done in your industry. You hire consultants that way: "Can you show me a case study that demonstrates how you have solved this problem before in our industry?"

> When it comes to innovation, I am bearish on bears and bullish on bulls. I think you should be too.

You hire employees that way: "I see here on your resume you have been working in our industry for quite some time. You must know Bill, Judy and Ralph. Those guys are brilliant!"

You build RFPs that way: "Please list other companies in our industry for which you have solved similar challenges."

Sometimes it is easier to appear ruthless when you are just being objective. The classic example is the CEO who comes in and does a reorg. They are able to look past personal relationships and make decisions based on job function and performance. Another example is an outside expert who dismisses a new technology because it is cumbersome. They don't know the people who have sunk their heart and soul into this technology for the past three years. You may have trouble being ruthless because you know too much about the possible implications of a tough decision.

You even choose your learning that way. You tell your employees: "Folks, I want each of you going to at least one industry conference and to join at least one industry round table."

And then the unthinkable happens: you get blindsided by "beginner's luck." Somebody who knows nothing about your business comes along and has the audacity to completely reinvent it.

iTunes? Beginner's luck.

NetFlix? Beginner's luck.

eBay? Beginner's luck.

Twitter, Cirque du Soleil, Mountain Equipment Co-op are examples of companies started by people with no industry experience. So was personal finance Mint.com and scores more we could mention (everything from Amazon to Zip Car).

THOSE IDIOTS BROKE THE RULES!

You could almost hear the things that people in the music, movie rental and auction business (just to pick three examples) were saying when iTunes, NetFlix and eBay came along. "What are these people thinking? Don't they know about the existing rules, the channel headaches, the legal hurdles, the technical hurdles, what's been tried before and failed, the demands of the sales agents, the way our products and services are purchased, the demands of our customers and their customers? ... "

Uh, no, they didn't. And neither will the competitor who will seemingly come from out of nowhere to upend your industry. And that is your takeaway.

"You can't read the label when you are sitting inside the jar" (see Chapter 4). This is how we like to describe the myopia that comes with being an expert. And odds are you are a myopic expert. That not only makes you vulnerable to people coming into your industry from the outside, it limits your ability to come up with revolutionary new products, and it often keeps you from making the decisions that, to others, may appear to be ruthless, but to an entrepreneur are just plain obvious.

"It says here, Miss, that you have abosolutely NO industry experience. When can you start?"

One solution? Think of intentionally infusing a bit of beginner's luck into your program. Here are a few ways you can do it:

Recruit for the challenge. Ask recruiters to look for a specific problem-solving ability instead of industry experience. Strive to hire leaders from outside your industry who have created the results you want in a unique way. For example, if you are being faced with disintermediation issues—and all service companies are—look for an expert who has tackled disintermediation. It's likely better that they know nothing about sump pumps or whatever your business is because it will enable them to solve your problem and challenge your paradigms. Beginner's luck.

Infuse outside experts. Every aspect of the innovation process can be enhanced by reviewing it through the eyes of experts from outside your industry "beginners." They will see things you don't see, get you excited about ideas you may pass over, and keep you from making the mistakes they've made trying to solve a similar challenge. Beginner's luck.

"Parallel engineer." We like to encourage this politically correct form of stealing. Send your peeps to conferences, learning events, retail establishments, other businesses, etc., that have nothing to do with your business. Have them talk to the experts there about problems you are having. Ask those experts how they have solved

similar challenges. Can you use this idea? Why invent a solution when one already exists?

Ask the newbies. Your newest hires and the youngest people in your firm carry with them what appears to be a look of confusion. It is actually the fleeting glow of a new idea desperately trying to be born. Ask them what they see. Ask them how they would solve the problems. Desperately try not to cut them off or offer your "expert" opinion. They just may give you an idea that will make you a hero.

From our experience, using these techniques will result in you being viewed by your competitors as a little bit crazy, a little bit ruthless and a lot-a-bit lucky.

Leaders lead. "Chance favors the prepared mind," Louis Pasteur said. So does innovation. If you want innovation to happen, you have to prepare the groundwork. You have to clear the way for those people who believe by getting rid of those who don't. Some call that ruthless.

I call it common sense.

(RING)LEADER To-Dos

Hire believers.

Fire the nonbelievers—consider the trade-offs of NOT firing them.

Listen to the youngsters—keep an open mind.

Frame the innovation language in your organization.

If you are burnt out and cynical, quit (you will be cured immediately).

Stop hiring leaders exclusively from your industry; ask the newbies.

(Cool fact: Most U.S. Presidents doodle. Want to be President? Perhaps you should doodle more. Begin here.)

Chapter 15

Taking the Lead

"Why should I follow you?"

When you introduce your vision of how your company can be more innovative, you may think employees will ask about cost, potential audience, probable success, how long will it take to get to market, and the like. And they will—out loud.

But the first (unasked) question that pops into their heads is going to be: "Why should I follow you?" By which they mean: "Why should I believe you are going to take us where we need to go?"

Even though they are (probably) not going to ask you those things directly, you need to answer their unspoken concerns before you do anything else. Otherwise, you are not going to get either their full attention or their best work.

So, how do you respond? My answer has three parts and I guarantee that if you put each into practice, you will become a much more effective leader.

1. Focus on the essential (not the important). It's easy to spend your time on the significant—for example, coming up with a new product to satisfy the salesforce's desire to keep having things to talk about. But necessary as that is, doing so isn't really going to inspire anyone.

STRATEGY is...
the art of sacrifice
– YES?

>> SO TRY THIS:
START your next leadership
team meeting by getting
everyone to generate a
"STOP DOING" list.

To-Die-For list

In contrast, creating a culture that celebrates failure—because if you don't take risks, you will never develop a game-changing product or service—is an essential belief that can shape everything your organization does. Here's another way of thinking about this: the important is rational; essentials are emotional. The important you put on a to-do list; essentials go on a to-die-for list.

2. Stay above the drama. Recessions/transitions/restructurings are, by definition, temporary. Understanding that is key to your ability to focus on the desired outcome and the kind of organization you want to build. The key question to ask: are you shaping the future or reacting to it? If you are just reacting, your organization will suffer. If you are always looking backward, you risk becoming a victim instead of a creator.

3. Lean into adversity and find opportunities. There will always be problems. The economy will go into a tailspin. A competitor does the unexpected and upends your market. Your customer will want something else. When this happens, don't hunker down or cut back. Instead, get more aggressive. Every adversity should be a trigger for you to encourage your team to find the upside or opening for your own innovative solution. Failure is OK. Inaction is unacceptable.

If you do each of these things, people will follow you.

SUPPORT IDEA PARENTING

You've seen this movie: You are involved in an amazing new product development program and you and the team deliver. You uncover a huge insight and hole in the marketplace that somehow your competitors have missed. The insight is so clear, the gap so big, that immediately product ideas to meet it begin to flow. You can even picture how this new product or service will look.

Your work is done. You leave the project glowing with pride.

Flash forward 12 months to the meeting where the next round of innovations to be launched are being unveiled. Your idea is presented, only it is not presented. It barely resembles the idea you helped conceive. What has happened to your beautiful baby?

I chose that baby metaphor on purpose.

Spend enough time around innovation and you become aware of a startling fact: ideas are just like children. Ideas need a loving set of parents to conceive them, encourage them, challenge them and protect them until they are ready to stand on their own. Good parenting will produce ideas—born as simple insights—that literally change the world. Good innovation is just like good parenting.

The problem is, as a rule, we as corporate executives/parents abandon our nurturing role too early. And just like in any family (or company), once the core set of parents is gone, the child/insight suffers.

The abandonment isn't deliberate—just a remnant of the way things used to be done. Despite all the talk about wanting to create "flat organizations," companies still have the bad habit of creating silos when it comes to research, marketing, R&D and sales.

BOINK!

As a result, insights are passed from department to department (from stepparent to stepparent, to continue our analogy) and are influenced and modified along the way. Thus, by the time your idea hits the market, it has been changed so much by so many people your customer will no longer recognize it as what they helped create.

The solution? The best companies establish a small, core innovation team—made up of all the key departments necessary to take a product from idea to marketplace (so yes, finance and manufacturing people are on the team)—that stays with the insight all the way from discovery to launch.

This approach works for three reasons: the team is small, it is focused and it is empowered. It has a budget, complete authority to make the project happen, and unlimited access to any part of the organization—including the executive leadership team. Having the original parents in place all the way to market ensures that the insight lives in the idea as well as the business, marketing and sales strategies.

As parents, we imagine our children someday walking down the aisle. On the day that they do, we will have been there for them every step of the way. We will have done everything that we could to encourage, protect and challenge them to be the best they could be. And when they are successful, we'll know that we've had more than a little to do with it.

Ideas are just like our kids. They deserve good parenting, too.

DEAL WITH THE BRILLIANT NAYSAYER

"What if Harold doesn't approve?"

And with these five words, discussion of a potentially brilliant idea comes to a screeching halt.

Most every company has a Harold (or Harriet). Typically, he has been with the company for 20-plus years. He knows more about industry norms, the company's intellectual property, interoffice politics and the CEO's family than anyone in the building.

And, unfortunately for you, good old Harold can effortlessly—and with absolutely no intended malice—recite four to six reasons why your idea won't fly. He'll tick down a veto list that may include chemical theory, union issues, patent law, an MIT-funded research study from the 1940s and two similar ideas that failed in 1985.

Everyone loves Harold. He's charming, remembers everyone's birthday and is willing to lend a hand. But at times, everyone also hates Harold because at a brainstorming session he is, unwittingly, at his worst.

He will sit with his arms folded and jaw clenched and wince at just about every idea. He'll often say things like: "I am trying to be really open-minded here, but ... " and eventually the air will leave the room as Harold explains in detail why the idea in question won't work.

His heart is pure. He isn't objecting for the sake of objecting. In his mind, "somebody has to keep failure from happening around here," and that somebody is him.

> "Named must your fear be before banish it you can."
> —Yoda

Harold doesn't know it, but he is often single-handedly keeping your company from moving forward. So how do you deal with the Harolds of this world? Here are five proven techniques:

1. Stop denying Harold exists. Awhile back, we were asked by a retailer to come up with new things it could offer that would  be consistent with the brand yet boost margins. During the kickoff meeting, it became apparent that there was a high-ranking Harold on the leadership team, but the CEO assured us she could control Harold and that we should not modify our process in any way.

Fatal mistake. At seemingly every turn, Harold found a reason why things would not work. Despite nudges, begging, sucking up and private conversations, nobody could keep Harold from "helping" things stay off track. It was brutal. Ideas were dismissed before they got enough attention to make them viable. This experience showed me that it is a much better strategy to embrace Harold. Start the project by having a private stakeholder meeting with Harold to fully understand and show you value his point of view and expertise.

2. Play by (some of) his rules. To be successful, an innovative idea must meet the criteria of company leadership. If you have a Harold, he qualifies as company leadership. In fact, his voice may be more powerful than the CEO's, since often the CEO will passively check in with Harold on all major initiatives.

Make sure you go to Harold and get an extensive list of criteria from him. What qualifies as a good idea? What technical challenges must we overcome? What operational hurdles are deal breakers?

Allowing Harold to set some—and agree to (almost) all—success criteria enables you to neutralize him. You can show him that you are creating and eliminating ideas based on his wishes. He can take credit for the ideas since his criteria are helping to shape them.

3. Learn from experts (fight fire with fire). If you bring in Harold's peers from parallel industries, they can share with him emerging technologies, new techniques, new discoveries and new ways of looking at old challenges.

What's a parallel industry? One that does the same thing you do, but is in no way competitive. Here's an example. You're in lawn care? You are offering products that protect and restore (healthy grass). What companies offer similar benefits, but for different things? Makers of hair care and skin care products. You invite experts from those fields who are just as technically qualified as Harold to help you.

We've done that through expert roundtables, lectures, field trips and online techniques such as Webinars and virtual roundtables. The results have been nothing short of stunning. You might expect Harold to be offended or feel challenged by the import of outside expertise, but our experience has been that these techniques are invigorating and liberating for him. One of our Harolds left an expert roundtable with 17 *(seventeen!!!)* pages of notes. Harold doesn't feel threatened because these experts aren't directly in his field. Besides, they're really smart—like him!

4. Arrange closed meetings with experts. What's also effective with the Harolds of the world is having them work alone with the outside experts. No one else allowed. For one thing, it appeals to his ego. (We are only having the most important people meet.) And for another, if there are only peers in the room, communication tends to be easier and more candid. These outside experts can help Harold by challenging his prejudices.

5. "Harold, this is an intervention." If the above strategies don't work or you no longer have the willpower left to make them happen, just put this on Harold's desk:

HEY LEADER, LOOK IN THE MIRROR

It is easy to blame chief executives and senior management for not devoting enough attention to introducing new products, but that is too simplistic an explanation for why radically new products are so rare. Us regular Idea Monkeys deserve some of the blame for at least four reasons:

Harold,
This message is from someone in the company who cares. I'd tell you who I am, but frankly I am afraid you might misinterpret this note as something other than an act of love or great respect.

First of all, I want you to know that you are really, really, reeeeeeaaally smart. I learn from you every time we are together.

I just wish, like the superhero that you are, you would use your powers for innovation good, not evil. Tell us how to construct new ideas – don't tell us why they won't work.

Anonymous

Successful, strategic innovations need more than a great idea. There's no shortage of new product concepts. We are willing to bet you could come up with a handful of intriguing ones in an hour if you set your mind to it.

But new ideas by themselves are worthless. You need to move from idea to execution, and that is where the majority of companies stumble. You need a new product development process—one that is codified, efficient and repeatable, and one that allows you to turn a notion into something you can sell.

But there aren't a lot of marketers who have tried to formalize a new product introduction. Too often, marketers see their job as simply coming up with the idea. They leave the actual development and production to someone else and then profess to be surprised when the finished product is not exactly what they had envisioned (see Idea Parenting). It is always nice to have someone else to blame when something goes wrong—such as, the product didn't sell. But it isn't the best use of your time or of company resources.

There is a shortage of Renaissance men (and women). This builds off the previous point. As we have seen, there are two distinct components to developing a successful new product: coming up with the idea and then putting it into practice—i.e., executing it. We must make sure that it is produced exactly as designed and that the marketing that follows is consistent with the overall message the product is supposed to communicate. Failure can arise when we look for people who possess both skills. Such people are extremely hard to find in any organization. Most people are naturally better at one or the other part of the process.

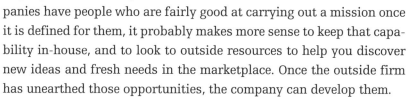

Instead of looking for someone who is good at both, it would seem more efficient to let people do what they do best. Since most companies have people who are fairly good at carrying out a mission once it is defined for them, it probably makes more sense to keep that capability in-house, and to look to outside resources to help you discover new ideas and fresh needs in the marketplace. Once the outside firm has unearthed those opportunities, the company can develop them.

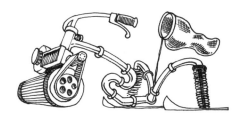

We tend to be fatalistic. As marketers, we seem to go into new product introductions with the expectation that we are going to fail. So we deal with new product failures, like the way an overweight person does with their problem: we periodically make half-hearted efforts to fix things … and then give up.

Just like someone who resigns himself or herself to being overweight, we conclude that there is nothing we can do to improve our batting average when it comes to introducing new products. Instead of throwing up our hands and saying "woe is me," we should be studying our past successes to see what we should do the next time we introduce something new.

That, of course, takes us full circle, underscoring as it does the need to have a replicable process to make new product development as painless as possible.

Blaming the CEO and others for not being more supportive about new product development is a waste of both time and mental energy. Look in the mirror and try to figure out how to make things better. Addressing the four problems we just talked about is a good start.

(RING)LEADER To-Dos

Remember to ask the question of yourself that everyone is asking: **"Why should I follow you?"**

Focus on the essentials (not the important).

Make a "stop-doing" list before you make a "to-do" list.

Stay above the drama.
A) Start with the question, "What is the outcome you want?"
B) Then answer it. Finally, make sure A and B are aligned.

Lean into adversity and find opportunities.

Avoid situations of idea abandonment. Idea parenting increases the odds that concepts will grow up healthy and eventually be successful in market.

Learn how to work around Harold. Stop denying that Harold exists in your company; play by (some of) his rules, but lock him into documented success criteria; let industry experts tell him he's wrong and open his eyes.

GRATEFULNESS; NAME THREE PLACES YOU ALWAYS FIND TREASURE.

> _____
  _____
  _____

> _____
  _____
  _____

> _____
  _____
  _____

Chapter 16
How To Witness Serendipity

Have you ever noticed how great things always seem to happen to the same people over and over again? I did, so it made me think hard about the concept of serendipity. For you who love trivia, Horace Walpole coined the term *Serendipity* in 1754, as he wrote about a "silly fairy tale" from his youth, *The Three Princes of Serendip*. The story is about three heirs to the throne who frolic around the countryside while good things just seemed to happen around them.

As a kid, I was fond of saying, "man, are you lucky!" I'd say it whenever something good happened to a friend. As an adult, I very rarely use the phrase anymore because after hanging out with so many highly innovative people, I've become aware that the luckiest people to most, aren't actually lucky at all. As Louis Pasteur said: "In the fields of observation, chance favors only the prepared mind."

Pasteur's quote makes perfect sense to (Ring)leaders. You work and work and work and work and eventually, when you get an opportunity, you are prepared. You seize the opportunity and make something of it.

Think about the luckiest person you know in business. Now think about how hard that person works. Turns out it isn't chance after all, but rather hard work that makes her "lucky."

For the Idea Monkey, a second quote rings true as well. This one by a really lucky fellow named Albert Einstein: "The most important decision a person will make is whether they live in a friendly universe."

You read earlier about the two shoe salesmen in a third-world country. After two weeks of selling, one complains that nobody wears shoes, the other sees that everybody *needs* shoes.

It seems that any situation can be interpreted as a wonderful opportunity or a tragic burden. These types of interpretations are happening every day all around you. Guess what? The lucky ones see opportunity where the unlucky ones see a problem. Said differently, if you complain a lot, you probably aren't that lucky. On the other hand, if you are always making lemonade out of lemons, our bet is that people see you as really lucky. If you want to reduce it to a formula, it would look like this:

Hard Work
+ Optimistic Outlook
"LUCKY Person"

BLESSINGS

In 2002, I lost a great friend to cancer. I will never forget picking him up just after he finished another round of chemo. It was summertime and I noticed Al was tearing up. When I asked him if he was in pain, Al said, "No, the truth is I was just smelling the cut grass. I didn't think I'd ever get to smell cut grass again."

To this day, I am grateful every time I smell cut grass.

From my experience, innovators are curious, hardworking and *grateful* people. They make their own luck through hard work and a healthy outlook. They savor and notice things that most of us take for granted. They literally stop and smell the roses and often thank God that they still can.

As a teammate, I try to attract, coach and encourage this kind of person and behavior. As a dad, I do a bit more.

PARENTING SERENDIPITY

We have a tradition in our family. When our kids are about seven or eight, we go on a treasure hunt. Since all kids are now researchers (thank you Google) we think it is important to dig where pirates once roamed. That's why our first treasure hunt was in Jamaica and our second was in Costa Rica.

The hunt starts when dad—that's me—mysteriously "finds" a map online. (A note of warning: constructing one of these maps nearly led to our Chicago office burning down on a Sunday afternoon. Adding burned edges to the map is a nice touch, but be careful!) In Costa Rica, we were trying to find the treasure of Captain Benito "Bloody Sword" Bonito, the "handsome" pirate who buried his treasure somewhere in Costa Rica around 1835. Here are a few lines from the Costa Rican map:

Look for the tallest of the trees that you spy,
Count ten paces to the ocean ye go
Then to the south twenty go by
Yer closer to me treasure than Ye know...

Every day on vacation, my sons and I stepped off the directions from the map. There were some challenges to overcome. First, we didn't know if Bonito was short or tall so we experimented with giant steps and baby steps. We also had to figure that 175 years was a long time ago so we were probably looking for trees that had fallen down. It was quite the challenge. Still we would choose our tree, or where we thought the tree might have been, step off the pace, and dig for about ten minutes.

And every day we'd fail.

On the last day of the vacation, after many, many failed attempts, we tried again. My son tapped something at the bottom of the hole and yelled, "It's the TREASURE!" The boys worked to pull out a small wooden box filled with coins from around the world. It was a glorious moment and a memory I'm hopeful that they will never forget.

Go to YouTube and search "Maddock Treasure" to witness the end of the treasure hunt or simply go to this address: http://www.youtube.com/watch?v=0BS0R0JWl64

Finding treasure is an amazing moment. In our business, we get to see the eureka moment all the time. When a team finally hits on an idea—a treasure—after sometimes years of digging, it is absolute magic. And from my experience, it feels the same whether you are eight or eighty-eight. Finding treasure is an ageless thrill.

Post script: Four years after older son Gunnar found his treasure in Jamaica, Cody found his in Costa Rica. With his teenage years clearly on the horizon, Gunnar stared at what his brother had found and you could see he was about to put pirates in the same category as Santa when I approached him.

"So Gunnar, why do you think we found the treasure?" I asked.

"Because we had a map?"

"Yes, when you have a proven process, a road map, you're more likely to be successful. What else?"

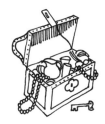

Gunnar thought for a moment. "Because Maddocks don't give up?"

"That's right. Try, fail, learn; try, fail learn; try, succeed, repeat. Never give up! Right? What else?"

At this point Gunnar was stumped. He thought for a moment and then said he didn't know. Besides, he could sense a lesson coming and was anxious to get on with it.

So I asked him, "Gunnar, we've been here for a week. Have you seen anyone else digging for treasure?"

He looked around. The beach was full of sunbathers, surfers and families. Nobody was digging. He shook his head and said, "Nope."

"Well Gunnar, I want to tell you something and it is really, *really* important. The people who are looking for treasure are almost always the ones who find it. So if you want to find treasure, be looking for it. And guess what Gunnar? There are treasures on every beach, in every room, in every relationship. My hope is that you go through life looking for them."

I hope you do, too. Your job as an Idea Monkey or a (Ring)leader is to find treasures or help others find treasures.

Keep digging. Be grateful. Be wonder-full.

—Mike